'*Struggles for Empowerment* offers a thoughtfu of the relationship between inequalities and higl lenses of Ireland and the region of Sindh in Pak seek to compare those two very different conte forces to produce a highly reflective account of their respective research journeys. They consider their engagement with theory and methodology and their common goal to make the voice of their participants heard, telling us stories not only about the persistence of gender and class inequalities but also about the potential of higher education to act as a driver of empowerment.'

**— Vincent Carpentier, Reader in the History of Education, UCL Institute of Education**

'This book is a valuable companion to all who wish to undertake ethnographic research with participants whose lives are generally concealed from view. Why are their lives hidden?'

**— from the Foreword by Eve Gregory, Professor Emerita, Goldsmiths, University of London**

# Struggles for Empowerment

*We dedicate this book to our parents*
*Zuhra Shaikh and Muhammad Shaikh*
*and*
*Tom (RIP) and Carmel Bruen*

# Struggles for Empowerment

## Higher education stories from East and West

Ambreen Shahriar and Teresa Bruen

is an imprint of

First published in 2019 by the UCL Institute of Education Press, 20 Bedford Way, London WC1H 0AL

www.ucl-ioe-press.com



British Library Cataloguing in Publication Data:
A catalogue record for this publication is available from the British Library

ISBNs
978-1-85856-896-6 (paperback)
978-1-85856-897-3 (PDF eBook)
978-1-85856-898-0 (ePub eBook)
978-1-85856-899-7 (Kindle eBook)



Typeset by Quadrant Infotech (India) Pvt Ltd
Printed by CPI Group (UK) Ltd, Croydon, CR0 4YY
Cover design by emc design ltd, using images © Dezignmart/Alamy Stock Vector (blue) and Agnieszka Murphy/Alamy Stock Vector (black)

# Contents

# Foreword

> Do not worry *Amma* [mother], let all the worries be mine.
> Forget about me. Think that you never gave birth to a daughter.
> Or think that the daughter to whom you gave birth is not linked
> to you anymore.

*(The words of Shabana, one of the participants in the book speaking to her mother at the time of her divorce, p.131)*

This book is a valuable companion to all who wish to undertake ethnographic research with participants whose lives are generally concealed from view. Why are their lives hidden? The simple reason is that the 11 people whose stories we share all descend from economically poor rural families in the Sindh area of Pakistan and in the Republic of Ireland. And, as such, their families' lives have mattered little, either in society at large or in social research. At first glance, any equation of poverty in the Republic of Ireland with that existing in Pakistan might seem paradoxical or even frivolous. On the one hand, rural Ireland is part of the European Union with advanced levels of social welfare and universal education; rural Pakistan, on the other hand, still permits a girl to be promised to a man in her first week of life and allows only minimal education to those who cannot afford it. Yet this unique collection of life histories of poor but remarkable people reveals patterns of similarity across 4,000 miles that intimately connect both groups.

The authors both address the following questions: What motivates mature students to continue their studies against all apparent odds? Why do so many students from lower socio-economic classes *not* continue with their studies? Why do some persevere? Are there common features shared between two very different countries? The answers to questions lie in the words of the participants themselves, skilfully unpicked by each author, using a common theoretical framework drawn from Bourdieu's *Outline of a Theory of Practice* (1977) of social and cultural capital, habitus, field and symbolic violence.

The structure of the book is unusual in a way that hints at many hours of conversation and planning by the authors. The four sections (Family and society; Our trajectories; Giving a voice to the unheard; and Towards emancipation and empowerment) take readers through the four sections of an ethnographic PhD study (the outer historical and social context; the role of the researcher in the research; the narratives or stories in the participants' words; and the analysis) and the chapters alternate between authors in each section. One way of reading the book is in chronological order all the way through to compare the two studies stage by stage. Another approach would be to read all the chapters by one author first in order to have a sequential and full picture of each study at a time. A third way would be to pick on a particular section, for example, Part 3, and to ask oneself: How would I think of analysing this data? before continuing to find out how it actually took place. Each approach to reading the book reveals new and unexpected insights.

Whatever way the reader might choose to read the book, it unravels the story of *struggle* common to all the individuals (and possibly many rural poor across the world) to attain higher education. As such, each individual awakens a deep empathy by the reader as we learn of the extraordinary sacrifices made by those whose lives are beset by the difficulties caused by poverty, as they learn to exert self-will and choice. Additionally, this is a methodology book, showing two examples of how Bourdieu's theories might be rigorously used in practice. Concepts of cultural and social capital, alongside economic capital and ideas of habitus and field are clearly explained and the stories of individual participants are meticulously unpicked throughout. In each case, the explanatory power of Bourdieu's theories is considerable. However, the analysis is situated clearly within a wider ethnographic approach where the passion of each author in choosing to conduct this particular research is obvious and permeates the whole endeavour. As the authors themselves conclude in their last sentence of the prologue: 'Yet they [the authors' studies] have a single shared aim: to break the silence and give voice to those who seek higher education and live unheard' (p.xi) As such, the book sees through the pessimism of the participants' surroundings to the success of gaining control over their lives. What emerges is a truly optimistic voice of hope for the future in both countries and contexts.

Eve Gregory
Professor Emerita of Language and Culture in Education, Goldsmiths

# Acknowledgements


## Teresa Bruen

The guidance of supervisors Dr Simon Warren and Nigel Wright were invaluable to me throughout this journey. Also my thanks go to Dr Gillian Klein for her support, guidance, patience and kindness.

## Ambreen Shahriar

Anyone who has read *The Monkey's Mask* (Kearney, 2001, 2003) can tell that this study is inspired by Chris Kearney. I would like to acknowledge Chris's influence. With the wholehearted support, both academic and personal, offered by Professor Eve Gregory and the ever so insightful guidance of John Jessel, my supervisors, my research journey became considerably easier. With the successful completion of my PhD, the next step was publication. After the viva voce, in which no correction/amendments were suggested, the examiners and supervisors recommended that I contact Trentham Books, and after a process of proposal reviewing, the extraordinarily helpful publisher, Gillian Klein, offered the wild idea of a joint book by myself and Teresa. We took the idea on board and here it is – our joint venture. Among many others, I would also like to thank Dr. Klaus Bung for his help in references from world literature in my chapters. With this book, I have made my little effort to give voice to my participants, who inspire me in hard times with their immense strength.

# Prologue

This is a story of inequalities of class and gender, of access and opportunity. It confirms that inequality is socially reproduced, and that economic circumstances divide society by class and gender.

Although the research for this book is based on studies in twenty-first-century Pakistan and Ireland, the stories they tell are not limited to these two contexts. As Kearney (1998: 310) notes, 'to some extent in the modern world, we are all exiles. We are all living in translations.' This statement is borne out by the studies from two entirely different contexts that together form the reality of this book.

'Culture is a complex entity which comprises a set of symbolic systems, including knowledge, norms, values, beliefs, language, art and customs, as well as the habits and skills individuals learn as members of a given society' (Hamers and Blanc, 2000: 198). Culture overpowers our minds. It is at the essence of our being. The research presented here deals with the culture of two different regions on the world map, cultures that differ from East to West; yet the similarities of experiences are remarkable and enhance our understanding of deprivation across the world. We discuss people's lives, with their problems and immense challenges from early childhood into adulthood, lives of struggle against all odds. These are discussions about how some people are still disadvantaged today, in the most developed times in history.

Centuries-old traditions and customs, patriarchal society, class division, gender division, religious bondages are only some of the key causes of unequal power in the world today. This results in the bifurcation of society into increasingly small and ever smaller groups, each differing from the others in a variety of ways and each dominated and dominant at the same time. And, as part of this story, this is our own struggle as researchers, pursuing higher education as a way to empowerment.

Access to and attitudes towards education are key issues in these struggles. Education in Pakistan, although free at primary and also secondary levels, is a privilege because the poor prefer their children to earn a living instead of 'wasting their time at school'. Socio-economic status is a major factor in acquiring education and gaining fruitful employment because good education is expensive. In Ireland, the recent drive to educate mature students is increasing the social participation of marginalized groups. Improving their social standing, as for their Pakistani counterparts, is an important motivation in their quest for education.

For many of our participants education was a remote option. Their society did not expect them to be educated and make much of their careers, considering, rather, that they have more important and urgent responsibilities: they must either support their parents by earning for them at a young age or bring up children, starting with their siblings, and do household chores. Education or pursuing a career is viewed as an extra responsibility, and thus never a priority. Moreover, as their social class decides whether or not they can study, education is the last thing on our participants' minds. The duties and responsibilities are carefully laid for each gender, yet there is no concept of their rights.

This book is based on two research studies conducted in different parts of the world: Pakistan and Ireland. Our studies are different, differently conducted, and based upon different research questions. Yet they have a single shared aim: to break the silence and give voice to those who seek higher education and live unheard.

# About the authors

*Ambreen Shahriar* has worked at the Institute of English Language and Literature, University of Sindh since 2004, and is currently Associate Professor. In 2007 she was awarded a scholarship to study in the UK. After an MA in Applied Linguistics and TESOL from the University of Leicester, she completed a PhD at Goldsmiths, University of London on issues of culture and identity with learners from deprived backgrounds. Dr Shahriar has remained a Research Fellow at Goldsmiths and this book has been written during her fellowship.

*Teresa Bruen* completed her general nurse training in 1987 in north London. She went on to complete her midwifery training in the Coomb Women's Hospital, winning the gold medal there. She completed an Hdip in public health nursing, a BSc in general nursing and a Masters in primary health care. After working in a community setting specializing in child development, she entered the field of education, completing a doctorate in education. Currently she is a lecturer and programme chair at Galway Mayo Institute of Technology, teaching psychiatric nursing and applied social care.

# Part One

## Family and society

1

As the two research studies discussed in this book are based on the issues of identity, poverty, gender, language, education, low esteem in the eyes of others and low self-esteem, it is important to understand the specific contexts to which they belong: Sindh, Pakistan and Ireland, particularly the West of Ireland. In the first two chapters we explain to our international readers what and how these two provinces are, discussing the history, culture, traditions, religious influences especially significant to education, and to people in general.

It is only by reviewing the history, culture, traditions and lifestyle in the two contexts that the reader can understand the disadvantaged position of our participants and appreciate the hardships of their struggle to break out of their position. To understand the attitudes and behaviours of our participants and the people around them requires understanding the culture and identity they carry as people. Through carefully considered reflection on the narratives of our participants comes a deeper holistic understanding of their educational trajectory and the struggle they endured to reach where they are today.

The first two chapters discuss the sociocultural contexts of our researches. They seek to show that the harsh and distressed conditions of the participants are due to the social scenario around them, which strongly affects their lives. One chapter discusses the history, culture, religion, tradition, language and education of Sindh, Pakistan, and the second, the scenario in Ireland. We hope this will help the reader understand the lives of the people in this book. It lends a backdrop to their narrative, thus contextualizing their stories.

*Chapter 1*

# Sindh, Pakistan: The people within their context

*Ambreen Shahriar*

> *Three major events have contributed to the shaping of modern Sindh's history, politics, and culture: the Muslim conquest in 711, the British conquest in 1843, and the Partition of India in 1947. (Pal, 2008: 2)*

Important events in the recent history of the subcontinent had a powerful impact on the lives of the people of Sindh. For centuries, Sindh enjoyed a significant and glorious position. Its language, culture and education system had been acknowledged and honoured during the British rule of India and even before that. However, after it became part of Pakistan, it was reduced to the dismal condition of a small province, struggling for its existence and its rights. Two-way migration between Pakistan and India at the time of Partition and the exodus of native Hindus left a hole in the educated population of Sindh, while the influx of *Muhajirs* created issues of culture and identity that affected Sindh more severely than any other province of Pakistan. The old language and culture are considered worthless in present-day Pakistan (see also Shahriar et al., 2014).

## Sindh: The history

Sindh as a country is mentioned in the *Mahabharata*, the ancient Sanskrit epic. Although its boundaries kept changing in different eras, it existed long before the time of the *Mahabharata*, during the days of the Kot Diji civilization (3000–2700 BC) and the Indus Valley civilization (the largest of the four ancient urban civilizations of Egypt, Mesopotamia, South Asia and China) of Moen-jo Daro and Harappa in 2500–1500 BC.

The province of Sindh has a very strong national identity, formed out of its centuries-old history, culture, language and politics, and carried by its people wherever they go. Sindhis have emphasized these identity markers since time immemorial, but these are losing ground in present-day Sindh (see Shahriar et al., 2014) and this is leading to a crisis.

According to Ahmad (1988), Sindh was, long before Partition, a magnet for immigrants and conquerors from all around India and beyond. Greeks (Alexander the Great), Iranians, Turks and Afghans all conquered

Sindh. Before Partition, immigrants who settled in Sindh were in the minority. They tried to integrate with the native population by adopting their language, culture and education system. Whenever Sindh was invaded by foreigners before Partition, Sindhis worked hard to maintain their identity; the invaders were absorbed by the natives and adopted Sindhi ways. After Partition, however, the immigrants – *Muhajirs* – came in large numbers, promoted their own faith, language and system of education, depriving the natives of their rights and making them a suppressed majority – aliens in their own land.

Sindhis – both Hindus and Muslims – form the majority of the population of the province. Siraikis, Balochs, Punjabis and Pathans/ Pukhtuns have been living here for centuries and have mostly integrated with the natives, adopting their language and culture and calling themselves Sindhis. This makes them different from the people who came to the province because of the Partition of India in 1947. After Partition, immigrants came not only from India but from provinces of Pakistan, and they did not try to integrate into the native culture. Therefore Punjabis living in the province before Partition are very different to those who came after, in both their lifestyle and their attitudes towards the province. This has fragmented Sindh, and the natives are searching for their identity.

The two-way migration took place in spite of the Pakistan Resolution (Lahore Resolution) of 1940, which was the basis of Partition and decreed that there should be no cross-border migration. The 'fathers' of that resolution realized that the formation of two countries, one for Hindus and one for Muslims, would cause Muslims from all over India to migrate to Sindh (and of Hindus in the opposite direction, from Pakistan and today's Bangladesh to India) and that such migration would cause enormous problems for the natives of those territories – the Sindhis, Bengalis and Balochs. Consequently, the Muslim leaders accepting the resolution decided that no cross-border migration would be allowed, and Muslims living in India should stay in India.

In the event, this decree was ignored, and in 1947 Muslims and Hindus, in huge numbers, crossed the border in both directions, causing untold misery and violence.

Though all these immigrants of 1947 speak Urdu as their first language, they can easily be divided into two groups: those accepting themselves as Sindhis because they are now part of the province and those still considering themselves as *Muhajirs*, demanding a separate province for themselves carved out of Sindh. *Muhajirs* form the biggest and most powerful Urdu-speaking pressure group in the province (Rahman, 1996: 112) and live mainly in urban areas, especially in the cities of Karachi and Hyderabad. After Bangladesh gained independence from Pakistan in 1971, a small number of Bihari-speaking people came quietly to Sindh. The Soviet–Afghan War in Afghanistan (1979–89) caused poor Pukhtuns from Afghanistan to come. They live mainly in Karachi, the largest city of Sindh, and gave the Urdu-speaking *Muhajirs* a hard time by competing with them for their rights – something the native Sindhis did not do to the same extent (see Gayer, 2014).

Immigration from Swat (Pukhtunkhwah) started with the earthquake in October 2005, and still continues as a result of the military campaign against the Taliban that unsettles the local population and turns them into refugees. Therefore Sindh is now home not only to existing communities of Afghan Pukhtuns but also to Pukhtuns from Swat (Pukhtunkhwah). This caused a power struggle between *Muhajirs* and Pukhtuns in the city of Karachi, and the native Sindhis became an insignificant minority in their capital.

There are other groups living peacefully in the province, including Bohris, Ismailis, Kachhi-Memons and Ahmedis. None of the immigrants who came during or after Partition tried to become part of the local community. Instead they retained their group identity, with aims and objectives different from those of the Sindhis. They were not concerned with the common good of the province as a whole, leaving the Sindhi natives alone in their struggle for the survival of Sindhi national identity.

During the campaign for independence before the Partition of India, some Sindhis were worried about Punjab's policies and, although most Muslim politicians supported the cause of Pakistan, others thought that Sindhis would become a minority which would be oppressed by Punjab (Ahmad, 1988). Accordingly, on 3 March 1943, the famous nationalist leader of Sindh, G.M. Syed (1904–95), presented a resolution in the Sindh Legislative Assembly which stated that the people of the subcontinent constituted not one but many nations. Therefore, claimed the resolution, Pakistan would not be a single 'Muslim nation' but a plurality of nations. This was ignored after the creation of Pakistan so that most ethnic groups were in danger of losing their identity. The resolution passed by Muslim and Hindu members demanded sovereignty and autonomy of the states (units or provinces) that were to form Pakistan. The Assembly declared that the distinct Sindhi identity had to be safeguarded and that Sindh was entitled to freedom from any power and parliamentary subordination to a central government or any other nation. Syed repeated this demand for the right to self-determination of the provinces to decide their own destiny along with their recognition as sovereign units; as a leader of the opposition in the Sindh Assembly, he met with a British delegation led by the Secretary of State for India on 2 April 1946. The demand clearly shows Sindhi concern for their culture and identity.

However, after Partition, the immigrants simply seized the land and buildings abandoned by fleeing Hindus, took over the major cities of Karachi and Hyderabad and occupied all important jobs in administration and elsewhere. The assault on Sindhi national identity continued when in 1948 Karachi was made the capital of Pakistan, and no longer constituted part of Sindh. Sindh was deprived of its biggest city and its cosmopolitanism, of a seaport and of a great source of wealth. Soon Sindh lost its autonomy and sovereignty and was treated as a little province that was subordinate to the bigger and administratively stronger province of Punjab. Finally, in 1955, the One-Unit policy came into effect, merging the former four provinces of West Pakistan (Sindh, Punjab, Balochistan and Khyber Pukhtunkhwah [then called North-West Frontier Province]) into one. This was to give the new amalgamated province greater power over Bengal, which would otherwise have been the biggest province. On all these and many other occasions, it was not the immigrants who faced the inclusion/exclusion tension but the natives of Sindh. Rahman (1996: 115) notes, 'Sindhi now became a major symbol of the sense of deprivation – cultural, educational, economic, and political – which Sindhi leaders and the emerging middle-class intelligentsia felt.'

## Sindhis: Before and after Partition

Markovits (2008) and Khuhro (1978) note that Hindus and Muslims were quite evenly divided in the province before and during British rule – most Hindus lived in the towns and most Muslims in rural areas. Both writers discuss the more educated and economically sound status of Hindus, who had formed an urban population and were either *amils* (government officers) or *banios* (rich traders and bankers who used to lend money on interest). Except for a small middle-class urban population struggling to survive, the rest of the Muslim population was rural. Muslim Sindhis were either *waderos* (landowners, who hired poor people to cultivate their land) or *haris* (the cultivators/peasants). On the one hand, there were rich Hindu Sindhi *banios* who lent money to Muslim *waderos*, and on the other hand, there were Hindu *banios* in villages as shopkeepers who also lent money, groceries and goods to *haris*, charging interest.

'The Balochi rulers of Sindh and their land-owning followers, both Sindhi and Balochi, known in Sindh as the *waderos*, were very dependent on the literary and financial skills of the local Hindus' (Markovits, 2008: 47). As the power shifted to the British, the *amils* easily acquired the administrative jobs under British rule whereas, despite there being a well-established British treasury system, the *banios* remained popular with the local *waderos*. Thus Hindus and Muslims lived in harmony in the province, without religious conflict, respecting and even celebrating each other's religious festivities, and practicing certain beliefs together as well. At the time of Partition, most of the Hindu Sindhis, who formed around 25 per cent of the population of Sindh, left for Far East Asian countries such as Singapore, Malaysia, Indonesia, Thailand and Burma, where many of them already had strong business links, and settled there. They left a vacuum in the educated urban Sindh community which could not immediately be filled by rural Sindhis. Thus, in the urban areas, positions of importance in government were left to immigrants, towards whom the government was sympathetic. The first Prime Minister of Pakistan, Liaquat Ali (1895–1951), was himself an Urdu-speaking immigrant from India. Unlike the government of India, the government of Pakistan allowed the immigrants to take possession of the properties abandoned by the Hindus in Sindh, so immigrants became wealthier than the locals almost overnight. At that time, the ordinary Sindhis left behind after the emigration of the educated Hindus lacked the power and education to challenge these issues.

The refugee groups who came to Pakistan under wretched conditions and whom the indigenous nationalities had wholeheartedly welcomed in the spirit of their common bonds of Islamic brotherhood, began to show a conflict of interest. They treated the indigenous nationalities as uncivilized and infidel peoples, blaming them for their Hindu historical past. This has been especially true in Sindh and Baluchistan, resulting in the persistent sense of regret among the locals (Kazi, 1987: 28–9).

The insistence of the indigenous elite on a secular society and the Sindhi demand for assimilation of the refugees into the local culture led to a hostile environment in the province.

Anti-Urdu and anti-*Muhajir* feeling among the natives of Sindh were exacerbated by, for example:

- the pro-Urdu policies of the government
- the concentration of *Muhajirs* in urban Sindh
- the dominance of *Muhajirs* in jobs in Sindh
- the demand for separating Karachi, Hyderabad and the surrounding areas from Sindh and turning them into a separate province for *Muhajirs*

- the relocation of the University of Sindh from Karachi to less developed Hyderabad
- the creation of the University of Karachi with Urdu as the sole medium of instruction, forbidding the use of Sindhi for answering examination questions.

As a result of more recent changes at administrative levels, Sindhis 'have also lost the right of education and employment in their capital city, Karachi, on the basis of being outsiders in the city ... they are hardly given 1/6th of what they pay to the Centre in the form of tax and other economic gains' (Joyo, 2005: xx).

In today's Sindh, the rural and urban divide is stark: rural areas are deprived of even the basic necessities of life. Most of the rural areas are still inhabited by Sindhis (both Hindu and Muslims) and the *waderos* are usually Muslims and omnipotent in their villages. For their people they are the rulers. It is the *wadero* who decides the fate of all the people in the village, including what jobs they would take, who the people would vote for in the country's general elections, who would stay in the village and whether villagers would send their children to school or not.

Even the village school cannot run if the *wadero* is not willing. Most of the *waderos* are not very interested in the progress of the people because they fear that if they are educated, they will eventually challenge them.

There is no middle class in rural areas. The *wadero* is upper class. The *haris* and labourers are lower class. The lower-class men have usually four job options:

- to work as *haris* on the *wadero*'s land
- to work as servants for the *wadero*
- to work on their own land if they have any
- to work as a labourer in the nearby town or city in a factory or on building sites or as navvies building roads.

In a few villages there may be a government-appointed doctor. He/she would be a native of the village and used to its conditions, so it would be easier to survive in the village, and it is likely that his/her spouse would be from the same village. Alternatively the doctor might commute to the village every day from a nearby city because living conditions in the villages are so primitive.

Consequently, only the children of the poor would attend a village school, if there is one. The school teacher would be someone from the village who has studied a few classes and passed exams taken for a BA as a private student without going to university (similar to distance learning in the UK). A village primary school teacher, usually male, would ask the *wadero* to get him a job, although for a poor salary. He would do nothing against the wishes of the *wadero* who got him the job as the *wadero* has power over whether the school operates or not.

Although the poor in urban areas are deprived, too, they don't have a *wadero* to turn to, including for decisions on education and work. Schools lack basic resources, such as chairs, desks, blackboards and books. They might have no water; their toilets might be in a deplorable condition. There might be no school building, and sometimes no teacher. The physical living conditions in the villages are not pleasant. There is no clean water, paths are muddy, especially during the rainy season, and there are no roads or toilets. Insects, especially mosquitoes, spread diseases in these unsanitary conditions and annual floods exacerbate the hardship. Students who study at home have to travel to nearby towns to sit for exams. The urban poor, too, suffer, but living conditions in cities are far better in comparison to those in rural areas.

## Religion in Sindh

Prehistoric Sindh was a primitive communist community. Sumerian, Semitic, Babylonian and Egyptian people admired Sindh, with its ideals of peace, harmony, collective property, personal and communal cleanliness, aesthetic sense (dance, music, painting, jewellery, toys and sculpture), education and a developed system of agriculture (Siraj, 2009). For hundreds of years, Sindh was invaded by outsiders: Greeks, Iranians, Sythians and others, but none could curb the artistic and architectural character of the region. 'Yet what Tatars did to Baghdad and Alexander to Iran was done by Arabs to Sindh, as they thought it to be their religious duty to destroy the pre-Islamic, which they thought to be un-Islamic', records Siraj (2009: 16).

However, Sindh remained a secular land for centuries after the Arab conquest and followers of different religions have lived here peacefully together. Sindh is the land of the Sufis, the mystics who taught the lesson of love and harmony to their followers. All natives of Sindh, whatever their religion or denomination, respect and follow the teachings of the mystics. Discussing the beliefs of the Sindhis, Syed (1974: 36) remarks that 'for Sindhis, spiritualism and atheism are only two sides of a picture' (author's translation; original: دھریت ۽ روحانیت ـ ھڪ تصویر جا ٻه رخ آھن). He goes on to say,

> *Henan (Sindhin) jadenh dahriyat aen jumli mazhaban khe hik tasweer ja ba rukh samjhyo ho ... ta he mazhaban je nale mei*

> *manhun mei nafaq nafrat paida karan khe kean thay berdasht karey saghya!!!* [In Sindhi language, Roman script].
>
> [Translation] They (Sindhis) viewed religion and atheism as two sides of a picture ... then how would they consent to intolerance and extremism in the name of religion.

The *Muhajirs*, however, consider religion to be their most important asset. They acquired a homeland, Pakistan, in the name of religion. That is why they disparage everything Sindhi as un-Islamic, be it language, culture, rituals or ideology. Thus, there is religious extremism in the areas where they are in the majority and a dislike of the Sindhi tolerance for all religious groups. *Muhajirs* discourage Sindhi ideas of harmony and peace and regard Sindhis as bad Muslims and bad Pakistanis. They are supported by the Punjabi ruling elite, who welcome the intolerance of the *Muhajirs* because they stir up religious divisions. Linguistic and religious discord make it easier for them to dominate the remaining three provinces, in accordance with the maxim 'divide and rule', learnt well from their colonial masters.

## Language in Sindh

The preferred language in Sindh is Sindhi; that is, the language in which Sindhis feel at home and which they find the best language for expressing their emotions. But Urdu has enormous prestige, and Sindhis will therefore use it if they know it and when they want to make an impression or show off their education or when talking to non-Sindhi speakers.

During the British era, a British official had to pass exams in Hindi-Urdu (then known as Hindustani) to be posted to any of the Indian provinces. In Sindh he had to pass a similar test for Sindhi, too. Sindhi was used in the domains of power and education before Partition. This is no longer so and is sorely missed.

Urdu has been considered a prestigious language and better than the indigenous languages in Pakistan, exceeded only by English in status and importance. Of all the indigenous languages, Sindhi is the only well-established language that has its own script. Language controversies are more prevalent in Sindh than in the other provinces of Pakistan because of the strong presence of Urdu-speaking immigrants from India since Partition, who began asserting their separate identity during the late 1980s (Rahman, 1996, 1999). The language riots in Sindh in the 1980s claimed thousands of lives and forced Sindhis to migrate from bigger cities to the safety of smaller towns and villages.

The Pakistani ruling elite, comprising mostly Punjabis, with an all-powerful position in administration, bureaucracy, the armed forces and legislature, support Urdu over their mother tongue and English over even Urdu. Rahman assumes that Punjabis do not support their language because they do not want the other indigenous languages to be strengthened. Rahman (1999: 98) says about the Punjabi ruling elite: 'Urdu gives it a wider base of support, a wider area to rule and seek jobs in, than the Punjabi itself' [sic]. Sindhis, however, made it clear that they never made Sindhi subservient to Urdu, although before Partition, they, like all Indian Muslims, supported Urdu over Hindi. Because of such sentiments, Sindhis are accused of being anti-Pakistan and anti-Islam (Rahman, 1996). Sindhis in turn believe that Punjab, being the majority province and having a more powerful status in the politics of the country, tries to reduce the distinctiveness of the other provinces through its Islam and Urdu propaganda (see also Kazi, 1987).

In this power struggle, Sindhis in rural areas can only communicate easily in Sindhi, a language they are proud of (like Swiss Germans who proudly speak Schwyzerdütsch among themselves but use High German as a prestige language). By contrast, in Pakistan, there are the native speakers of Urdu who speak Urdu well, and the Punjabis whose native language is Punjabi but who also have a tradition of sometimes speaking Urdu among themselves because Urdu is a prestige language, an 'educated language'. When Sindhis speak Urdu, their distinctive accent is often ridiculed. Kazi (1987: 48) records that an official effort was taken by the civilian government of Zulfiqar Ali Bhutto (1971–7), 'that provided Urdu-speaking refugees a period of fifteen years to learn Sindhi [and assimilate into the native population]'; until that time no discrimination was to be laid on grounds of language. They were to be called 'New Sindhis'. But the Bhutto government was soon overthrown by the military regime of General Zia-ul-Haq and 'the assimilation programs came to a halt'.

## Education in Sindh

Sindh has been a centre of learning since prehistoric times. With the invasion of Kot Diji civilization (3000–2700 BC) its two towns of Kot Diji and Gomla were burnt down. Owing to this tragic end, scholars have been unable to reach conclusions regarding educational provision in this early Sindhi civilization, except that it was agrotechnical, so met the immediate needs of those early Sindhis. A recognized education system was found in Sindh as early as the time of Moen-jo Daro (2500–1500 BC), with a 'pictographic script' of the Sumer civilization, which had developed beyond the early stage of pictography. Although Aryan invaders destroyed much of this early Indus civilization, they adopted the local tradition of learning, although they superimposed Sanskrit over the local language of Sindh as the language of learning, as did the Arabs, the Arghuns and the British invaders later on.

Iranians, Greeks, Scythians, Kushans, Turkoman Parthians, Epthalites and White Huns continued to invade Sindh one after the other. They usually merged into Sindhi culture and tradition and lost their own identity, and they all continued to uphold the local system of education. When the Arabs conquered Sindh, they found that the Holy Qur'an had already been translated into Sindhi. Siddiqui (2006: 7) quotes the famous Muslim scholar Ibn Abi Sabeeya as having written that the Sindhi people had a storehouse of knowledge that was later transferred to Greece.

Sindhi is the only developed and well-established provincial language in present-day Pakistan, since it was the medium of instruction in Sindh during British rule and before. It was also the only language to be affected by the introduction of Urdu as the medium of instruction from Year 6 in all government schools during the 1950s (Rahman, 1999). During different regimes the provinces have either been allowed to teach and use their local languages or have been prohibited from doing so. This badly affected the Sindhis, who could have adopted Urdu or English (although it would have been unjust and difficult to impose) if the policy of the successive governments had remained the same. However, primary and secondary education in rural Sindh is given in Sindhi, which is the medium of in-class communication. Yet a string of bills was passed that reduced the use of Sindhi in education. Whereas formerly Sindhi was compulsory for all people living in Sindh, including Karachi, its capital, at SSC (Secondary School Certificate), an exception is now made for Karachi where Sindhi is excluded from the syllabus. This is extraordinary when one considers that Karachi is the capital of Sindh. Such policies are designed to suggest that Karachi is not part of Sindh. When Urdu-speaking people from Karachi chat with people from the rest of the province, they might say: 'We are from Karachi and you are from Sindh', in an effort to separate the two. The language policy about the status of Sindhi in Karachi is part of such separatist tendencies. In the private schools catering for the elite throughout the province, English is the sole medium of instruction. Thus the population is divided into groups with varied proficiency in different languages.

The education system in Pakistan generally allows and encourages cultural transmission on a hierarchical basis – private schools for the rich and public schools for the poor – resulting in underprivileged children lacking access to better education. It conceals differences of distribution, consumption and accumulation of cultural capital (Bourdieu, 1984) by providing a single procedure of selection in the job market. People from underprivileged sociocultural backgrounds try to achieve a place in society in which such rules are laid down by the privileged classes, so they have little hope of anything more than survival. All the parties involved in this power struggle, including the dominated class, agree to these rules unquestioningly, thus legitimizing what Bourdieu (1984) calls symbolic violence.

Yet economics, not education, is the key concern of the people. Even those who belong to the highest class of society prefer their children to study subjects that could lead to financial advantage. Conforming to the mores of social reproduction, people usually expect their sons to adopt the same profession as themselves, so a businessman's son would be a businessman, a teacher's a teacher and so on. The education of girls is always secondary to the education of boys, even in the highest ranks of society. Parents usually dream about the professional success of their sons, whereas daughters may perhaps settle for being school teachers – it is of little account.

Poor people do not necessarily wish their children to be educated. During their education they will give no financial support to the family. Also, the acquisition of education might make their children think the family profession is lowly, and the parents realize that the job market is not welcoming to their children. This can cause both financial and psychological problems.

## Family life in Sindh

Ancient Sindh was a matriarchal society with a woman the chief of the clan, the inventor of agriculture, the mother of all creation, a goddess (Siraj, 2009). The woman was the head of the family and the man was the breadwinner. A fine line divided the roles between genders then. Today, too, the rights and responsibilities of the two genders are divided, along with the expectations from each; although class imposes a finer division than gender in today's Sindhi society.

Sindhi society divides social spaces for men and women, yet it is not as conservative towards its women as some traditional South Asian communities. Though women are expected to follow their fathers, brothers, husbands and sons when making any important decisions, they are not expected to stay within the four walls of the house. With their modest dress and lowered gaze, they can go out of the home whenever and wherever needed, keeping in mind that they carry their family's honour with them. Covering the head and upper part of body with a Rao, a loose, long unstitched piece of cloth worn over clothes, or Chaadar, an even bigger piece of cloth worn when in public, is common among both Hindu and Muslim women. Purdo or Purdah, a veil covering the face, is the individual choice of the woman or her husband and family. Small girls can play outside their homes with boys from the neighbourhood without any restriction.

Respecting women is a general norm in Sindh society. Though they are not considered equal, women are definitely considered a symbol of honour for the family and are usually treated respectfully by men within and outside the family. Men and women, however well they know each other, address each other as *Ada* (brother) and *Adi* (sister). Sindhi men usually call little girls *Amma*, meaning mother. Though girls are respected, as in most of the Indian subcontinent, the birth of a girl is not desired. A son is considered a strong support for parents, an heir to their name (as daughters usually change their family name after marriage) and carries the family's honour. A daughter may inherit property but this is a matter of choice, and daughters are given a smaller share, if any. Therefore, unlike the old saying, 'A son is a son till he gets a wife, a daughter is a daughter all her life,' Sindhis believe that daughters have to get married to become members of their husbands' family, whereas sons remain in their own family all their lives and they bring wives who will fill the place of daughters in the family.

In today's Sindh, due to the prolonged economic crisis, both sexes usually have to earn a living. The conditions in poor families are especially concerning, where many children receive no education because they have to earn for their families, whereas those from the middle and upper class can first receive education and then work for their living.

In lower-class families both parents usually work as servants/maids in the village homes of their *waderos*, as servants/maids in the cities, in factories at the outskirts of towns and cities or at home doing embroidery and other handicrafts (usually made by women and the products sold by their menfolk).

Factories are on the outskirts of the towns, and often there are small satellite villages around them where the poor workers live with their families. Many families migrate to live near a factory, simply squatting on some vacant plot of land and erecting a shelter there. Many factories provide transport to bring the workers from their homes to the factory, so the parents working in factories can often live with their families. Their children also work during the day but some go to school. Young boys work in the fields, collect plastic, paper and other waste to sell for recycling, or work in shops or houses to earn money. Girls in poor families do embroidery and household chores from a very young age. Some women of poor families in cities have greater responsibility for earning a livelihood for their families than women in villages because their men often don't work, taking money from their wives, sometimes to gamble.

Everyone is expected to marry and have children. Marriage of girls is more problematic than of boys, usually due to the custom of dowry that prevails in not only poor but also middle- and upper-class families. In many cases, young girls are married to older men who demand no dowry, but 'bride price' is common among poor families. Ironically, the educated class consider bride price to be a custom of uneducated, backward people, yet it has not liberated itself from the custom of dowry. Similarly, second marriages by men for the sake of having sons or on the death of the first wife is common in rural areas, but it is rare for Sindhi women. Inadequate family planning leads to problems of poverty associated with large families. An uneducated poor couple might have between six and twelve children to support. Households can become even larger because parents and grandparents usually live together in an extended family. They might even be joined by a son or brother who cannot support his own family, perhaps owing to being physically unfit, mentally unstable, a gambler or drug addict. People do not question whether people with mental problems or bad habits are fit to marry; instead parents expect such offspring to improve after marriage. In extreme cases this can impose an unbearable burden on the one person who has to earn a living for all. Therefore children are encouraged to work rather than go to school, even though schooling is free for all at primary and secondary level – if it is available.

Sindhis, regardless of class division, still live as extended families. In rural areas, the extended family usually lives within a compound building with sections for each family unit. In urban areas, where such big compounds are rare and difficult to manage, extended families prefer to live close to each other and stay together through thick and thin. Disputes within the family are solved by family elders and those between different families by village or community elders.

*Chapter 2*

# Ireland and education in context

*Teresa Bruen*

*Education is not the filling of a pail,*
*but the lighting of a fire.*

William Butler Yeats (1865–1939)

## A brief history

I don't pretend to be a historian, so my introduction to the history of education within Ireland will be brief. Some reflection on the past allows us to understand the present better (Skehill, 2007), and I hope this outline will cast light on the educational trajectories of the mature students my chapters are about.

The delivery of education in Ireland has traditionally been the domain of the Roman Catholic Church and an inextricable link between religion and education remains. But this is slowly changing as Ireland moves hesitantly towards becoming a secular state. The Roman Catholic Church was, and still is, the largest religious denomination in Ireland, with 78.3 per cent of the population declaring themselves to be Catholic.

Education at primary and secondary level was delivered in Catholic schools with a strong religious influence and the children were taught by nuns, priests and brothers. The Church of Ireland schools were also run by the religious, providing education to children of the Protestant faith.

From 1831, primary education was free, funded by the British government. Each church set up their own parish schools that were managed by the local parish priest or, in the case of the Church of Ireland, by their minister. Protestant and Catholic children attended their own religious schools and absolutely did not mix. There was an element of mistrust between them, with each religion firmly entrenching their religious beliefs and traditions in their pupils. Each religious denomination was concerned with protecting against any chance of children and families being converted away from their faith.

At that time, children would have left school at the age of 10 or 11 to work on the land. People were very poor and lived in harsh conditions, and the children were expected to find employment and bring in money to help support their parents and younger siblings. The education provided was very basic and was seen as of little value within their homes.

Secondary school education was not free. Parents had to pay for their children to attend boarding schools, which were also run by the religious orders. Most secondary schools were for boys and it wasn't until the 1880s that girls began to attend secondary schools run by nuns – a direct result of the increase in demand for educated women for middle-class jobs.

University education was exclusively the domain of the elite, prosperous and privileged. Until the 1840s Trinity College was the only university in Ireland. This was seen as a Protestant university and while Catholics and Presbyterians were allowed to attend, they were not allowed to teach or to avail themselves of any scholarships. As a direct result of this discrimination the Catholic bishops developed the Catholic University in Dublin. It was unfunded and could not award degrees so it was relatively unsuccessful.

After much lobbying, the British government passed the Royal University Act, which set up the Royal University. This was essentially an examining board. All students who so wished were able to sit their examinations and if they were successful they were awarded their degrees. It also supported scholarships, and fellowships could now be awarded to teachers who taught in the Catholic University.

And so Ireland has had to struggle in order to ensure that its citizens are treated fairly and can pursue education. Its troubled history and its difficult and complex relationship with education has been strongly linked with religion and in particular the Catholic Church. This still lingers today, with many schools under its patronage. Religion is taught in all schools and in the majority of primary schools the children are prepared for the sacraments of the Church, Communion and Confirmation, all of which encroaches on the hours provided for the core curriculum. There has been lively debate and an ever-growing discourse questioning the preparation of children for religious sacraments during the school day and the usefulness of teaching religion within modern schools. All this is not for discussion here, but it demonstrates the ever-changing, ever-evolving discourse around education in modern times.

Nonetheless there has been a steady increase in the number of multi-denominational and inter-denominational schools in recent years – a reflection of the changing ethnic landscape of Ireland and its evolving, diverse society.

## The Irish language revival

I cannot move on without mentioning the teaching of the Irish language within the school system at both primary and secondary level. After a troubled history, Britain departed Ireland in 1922, leaving a free state that needed to be developed by its own elected government. A part of this development was the strong move to look at not only economic and foreign policy but also, equally importantly, at the development and renewal of the Irish culture itself. At the heart of a country's culture lies its language. As part of this revival they looked to the schools and the education system as a whole. It was decided that for Irish to become part of the culture of the nation it must be taught in school. Consequently the Irish language was taught in the schools as a compulsory curriculum subject. The Irish Free State government regulated that Irish was to be taught in all primary schools for at least one hour a day. It is also a compulsory subject in secondary schools and remains so to the present day.

Currently there has been a growing movement within the primary school arena for all-Irish-speaking schools. This is where all children are taught all of their subjects through the medium of the Irish language. Presently over 53,000 children in Ireland attend a Gaelscoil (schools teaching through the medium of Irish).

> Is fearr Gaeilge briste, ná Béarla clíste.
>
> (Broken Irish is better than clever English).

## The discourse of widening participation

> *As a country we have everything to gain and nothing to lose by increasing levels of participation in Higher education among all our citizens.*
>
> Jan O'Sullivan TD (2015)

It is important for this book to explore the concept of higher education, its history, where we are today and the discourse of widening participation, particularly in relation to Ireland. This, I hope, will give deeper meaning to the narratives of the mature students I present and help us to understand their reflections and their stories within this context. Mature students in Ireland are defined as those aged 23 years or over on 1 January of their year of entry to higher education.

Historically, higher education was the privilege of a small sector of society. However, in Ireland and throughout Europe, there have been enormous changes and challenges surrounding the accessibility of higher education. The focus of widening participation has shifted from a small elite sector of society to expanded mass participation, now moving towards universal participation in higher education. There has been unprecedented growth in participation in higher education and this has presented many challenges. However, not all sections of society have benefited from widening participation initiatives; sections of society traditionally remain under-represented in higher education. These sections of society include those from poor and disadvantaged socio-economic backgrounds, and people who have disabilities. The focus of this enquiry is on students who are over the age of 23 when they commence their first year of study and who come from backgrounds that have traditionally been excluded from participating in, and thus benefiting from, higher education.

The field of higher education within the Republic of Ireland has been influenced by the economic recession. Ireland is currently coming through that recession but higher education remains poorly resourced and funded since the abolition of fees for all students. Higher education authorities have since had to source money to fund education and this has been a serious challenge. It has also led to an increase in registration fees for students attending higher education; the student body has seen their registration fee increase from €850 to €3,500, with more increases expected.

Nationally and internationally there are drives to provide equity of access to ensure that traditionally excluded groups are given the chance to access higher education. The National Plan for Equity of Access to Higher Education 2015–2019 (National Access Plan) identifies target groups as an overall strategy to promote and encourage participation. One of the target groups specified is mature students. Previously targets have only been developed for those mature students who intend to undertake a full-time programme. However, the National Access Plan has for the first time acknowledged the significance of those mature students who are undertaking programmes on a part-time and flexible basis, and have developed targets for this specified cohort too. This suggests the evolving nature of the delivery of higher education to ensure that all citizens may access it through a range of different spaces. Targets set by the National Access Plan (HEA, 2015) propose that mature students comprise 16 per cent of all full-time entrants (currently 13 per cent) and suggest that flexible/part-time provision will increase to 24 per cent (currently 19 per cent).

Contemporary Irish society recognizes the importance of higher education in the creation of a vibrant economy. Higher education is taking place within a rapidly changing economy and faces many challenges. In 2009, the number of new entrants to higher education was 42,500, but the Department of Education and Skills projections for the next 20 years highlight that demand will rise to approximately 65,000 in 2025. On examination of this projection it can be seen that the bulk of the demand will come from mature students, international students and a greater demand for postgraduate study.

Higher education is concerned with the advancement and pursuit of knowledge and is viewed as a valuable resource affording benefits for the individual and society. Trow (1973) describes the evolution of higher education as having three distinct phases. Firstly the elite phase where less than 15 per cent of the eligible age group participate in higher education. Secondly, mass participation rates which exceed 15 per cent but remain lower than 50 per cent. Thirdly the universal stage whereby participation reaches more than 50 per cent of the age group. The Irish system of higher education has increased its student population by approximately 2 per cent yearly since the mid-1960s, currently has an age participation rate of 57 per cent and is within the universal stage (OECD, 2006).

The concept of access equated with the citizenship right of certain social groups to participate in higher education was the genesis for the widening participation discourse. The considerable expansion of opportunities has centred round the provision of full-time higher education and the focus mainly on entrants who have recently completed secondary education. Across OECD countries, higher education students in the Republic of Ireland have the narrowest age range (OECD, 2009). A report commissioned for the OECD to examine the higher education system in Ireland in 2004 highlighted that mature students represented 2 per cent of the student population in 1998, and drew attention to the Clancy Report (Clancy, 2001), which emphasized the social disparity of the student population intake. Almost 100 per cent of the children of professionals and 64 per cent of the children of employers and managers entered the higher education system. Recent figures from the HEA (2015) show that the largest socio-economic group of full-time new entrants to the University and Institute of Technology sector is the higher professional group. This compares poorly with only 23 per cent of the children of unskilled and semi-skilled manual workers entering higher education (HEA, 2015). The largest proportion of full-time mature entrant respondents come from a manual skilled background and this contrasts with the non-mature respondents, whose largest socio-economic group is employers and managers (HEA, 2015).

The thread running through the widening participation (WP) debate is equality: ensuring access to higher education for under-represented groups. While there have been many political debates related to the field of higher education, these have focused on the structure of the sector, while the predominant sociological perspectives have influenced the empirical and theoretical concerns of WP research (Kettley, 2007). This has led to a reduction in accounts concerning the barriers to higher education, because of a failure to examine the relationship between students' social characteristics, their learning experiences and academic careers (Kettley, 2007).

Burke (2002) suggests that WP research concerns the relationship between higher education and social injustice. The agenda of widening participation research within Ireland is concerned with social inequality, an economic competitive market and financial constraints. The document *Towards a Future Higher Education Landscape* (HEA, 2012) acknowledges that there are two significant drivers for change: quality and participation. It states that, 'There is a significant tension between these two objectives which needs to be managed in a sustainable way' (HEA, 2012: 4). It suggests that policy and practice should support access to those who wish to participate in higher education.

Globally there has been a shift to a universal higher education sector that has been driven by specific policy changes and the growing focus (and this is true of Ireland today) on the under-representation of specific groups, particularly of mature students (Kettley, 2007; OECD, 2009). Blanden and Machin (2004) submit that there is inequality within higher education with expansion only benefiting children from relatively rich families. The reproductive rule of thumb is that a person's family background, for example parents' educational background, is useful in predicting achievements and career prospects (Bourdieu and Passeron, 1990; Bourdieu, 1988; Bowles and Gintis, 2002). In Ireland there has been an increase in initiatives to facilitate participation for traditionally marginalized groups (Shevlin et al., 2004). Current higher educational policy strives towards an inclusive educational system encouraging a diverse student population and setting out as its objectives a more flexible student-centred approach (HEA, 2015). The participation of mature students in higher education has increased; most of this increase has been on a part-time or flexible basis (HEA, 2015).

However, The National Strategy for Higher Education to 2030 (HEA, 2011) draws attention to persistent inequalities in Irish higher education. It states that there is a need

> for provision of educational opportunities that differ significantly from the traditional model, in which a student enters higher education directly after finishing secondary school, stays there for

> three or four years, enters employment and never again engages with the education system. (HEA, 2011: 35)

Behan and Shally (2010) report in the current manpower forecasting study that economic growth over the medium term will be greatest in occupations that require third-level qualifications or high skill levels. Projection forecasts for low-skilled occupations are predicted to reduce or experience only minimal growth. The conclusions of this forecast focus on the significance of a robust lifelong learning strategy that will enable people in the labour market to make their skills more appropriate to a changing employment market and to offer flexible programmes to individuals to enable them to achieve gainful employment. The literature proposes that the economic market is central to government policy, with the crucial role of higher education constructed as augmenting employability, entrepreneurialism, economic competitiveness and flexibility (Morley, 1999; Thompson, 2000; Burke, 2002; Archer, 2003; Bowl, 2001). This cannot become a reality without a strong focus.

Institutes of higher education within the Republic of Ireland have focused their attention on the recruitment and retention of mature students. This has been driven by the widening participation objectives, whereby students from non-traditional backgrounds are afforded an opportunity to re-engage with education through access courses. This is applauded within a democracy that values all citizens equally and believes in a just society. Access to higher education has become defined in terms of equity and the understanding that proactive policies and practices are needed to enable participation of those who have been under-represented. Nonetheless, *The National Strategy for Higher Education to 2030* (HEA, 2011) highlights Ireland's inadequate attempts at achieving lifelong learning. Currently 7 per cent of adults aged between 25 and 64 in Ireland participate in education and training – this is extremely low and needs further efforts to improve the numbers.

Without adequate investment in skills, people will remain on the fringes of society, technological progress will not convert into productivity and countries will no longer be able to compete in a knowledge-based global economy. Part-time and flexible learning opportunities are essential to increasing access to higher education and widening participation for adults who need to combine study with work or caring responsibilities and to ensure equity of opportunity and the enhanced benefits to individuals and to society as a whole (Fleming et al., 2010).

## The motivations of mature students

*Ambition can creep as well as soar.*

Edmund Burke, Irish statesman

The motivations of mature students who decide to enter higher education are complex. Little is known about how potential mature students weigh the personal advantages of studying and the attainment of a qualification with the challenge of managing to surmount perceived barriers to commence the transition process to becoming students (Osborne et al., 2004). Intrinsic personal development and a love of learning are the key threads in the literature exploring their motivations. However, economic rationalism, altruism and human capital theory are also common motivational reasons given by mature students for going into higher education (Reay, 2002; Osborne et al., 2004; Fleming and Finnegan, 2011). The influencing factors are classified into four categories: firstly, national policies related to recruitment, for example widening access and student finance. Secondly, economic and labour market conditions, which may vary from region to region. Thirdly, policy and practice of institutes of higher education and, finally, the personal background and circumstances of individual students. All four factors affect the overall decision-making process (Osborne et al., 2004). For many mature students the decision evolves over an extended period of time (Williams, 1997).

Flexibility in delivery of educational programmes is an important plus for mature students, particularly if the programme is vocational (Reay et al., 2002). The concept of human capital can be employed by mature students when they consider the motivations for entering higher education. They analyse the benefits of education, such as future occupational prospects, against their investment (Broomfield, 1993). A significant number of students undertaking part-time education in their thirties give enhanced career prospects as their main reason for higher study (Bourner et al., 1988); it is one of the main drivers for mature students. Woodley and Brennan (2000) and Woodley (2001) suggest that personal advancement is a crucial motivator when deciding to enter higher education. Consequently it is in keeping with the rational decision-making model by which those decisions are made to realize certain ambitions that are directly related to areas of employment or occupation (Davies et al., 2002). But it is not all about the money. Mature students identified developing knowledge and enhanced personal development as a common motivation for entering higher education (Cree et al., 2009).

Nonetheless it can be a daunting time for the mature student and entering the field of higher education proves to be multifaceted and the decision-making process 'fragile' (Davies and Williams, 2001). A great deal of consideration is undertaken by the potential mature student within the process. The decision to participate can bring with it a complete and utter change in their lifestyle, which may prove immensely challenging but also rewarding as we see.

Men give more practical reasons than women for enrolling in higher education (Osborne et al., 1984; Woodley et al., 1987). An interest in the area of study and a chance to enhance their career prospects and to improve upon their existing qualifications was also evident, as was the desire to change the direction of their lives. Finally identified was an ambition that they always wanted to engage with higher education but that the opportunities had not been there (Davies and Williams, 2001).

Across the board many mature students express the notion of wishing to contribute to the social world (Reay and Mirza, 1997). This is a key narrative of the mature students investigated by Reay et al. (2002), who spoke about wishing to give something back and make a difference by drawing on their own rich and sometimes difficult backgrounds to benefit others in society. Cree et al. (2009) found that three-quarters of their mature student cohort rated as important the concept of helping people. Thus values of altruism are clear motivators for entering higher education. Also, some mature students who were parents spoke about the significance of being a positive role model for their children and passing on their education, while also desiring a better lifestyle for themselves and their families through participation (Edwards, 1993; Reay et al., 2002).

While the motivators to enter higher education are significant, so too is the decision-making process. The literature suggests that the processes involved in deciding to enter higher education differ between the traditional students and those from a non-traditional background such as mature students (Davies and Williams, 2001; Reay et al., 2002). Mathers and Parry suggest that the decision-making process to enter higher education is 'qualitatively different for prospective traditional (e.g. middle-class school leavers) and non-traditional (e.g. working-class or mature) students' (2010: 1085).

Reay et al. (2005) discuss the implications of social class, ethnicity and gender that impinge on mature students and their importance when choosing a higher education institute (HEI). Osborne et al. (2004) report how the mature student weighs up their options before they become a 'decider'. After making the decision to enter higher education, they organize finances and domestic responsibilities and then become an 'applicant'.

The *National Strategy for Higher Education to 2030* (HEA, 2011) acknowledges the increasing demands from adults to engage with higher educational opportunities that are appropriate to their needs. It highlights that this demand will increase in line with higher unemployment and the vulnerability of current employment opportunities. Consequently, it accepts that adults who are unemployed will need to have appropriate educational and training opportunities to update their existing knowledge and skills. Those who remain in employment will need the opportunity to retrain and advance their knowledge. The generation of flexible programmes is recognized as crucial by the Higher Education Authority (HEA, 2015). It highlights that the flexibility of programmes should be viewed as a key indicator to responding to the needs of Irish society and should benefit from equitable funding supports.

Inherent within the choices accessible to mature students in relation to higher education are the financial supports available. Currently in Ireland mature students who wish to engage in higher education do not have fees to pay. However, students must pay a yearly registration fee that has significantly increased since its introduction in 2008 (initially €850 annually but €3,500 in 2015). There have been suggestions by the academic hierarchy to reintroduce fees, as HEIs are finding it increasingly difficult to deliver a service that is so poorly resourced.

The individual circumstances of each mature student influences their entire decision-making process. Studies reveal that geographical location is a key indicator for mature students when choosing an HEI (Reay, 1998; Ball et al., 2000; Wright, 2011). Time is a valuable resource and cannot be wasted in travelling to and fro. Reay et al. (2001) found that mature students are time-poor and therefore have to be pragmatic. Primary considerations identified by the mature student population were the financial and material constraints, including the cost of travel (Reay et al., 2002). Time implications ensured that students carefully considered the geographical location of the HEI and whether there were direct lines of transport. A mature student who has domestic and caring responsibilities that are not normally the realm of the traditional student will want to pay for the least possible time for childcare (Wright, 2011).

Also pertinent to the decision-making process was the notion of fit and identity within higher education itself. Mature students identify the need to hold on to their identity, explicitly stating that they needed to be themselves and not pretend to be someone else (Mathers and Parry, 2010).

The literature highlights the difficulties in transitions that mature students encounter in relation to identity and fit as they negotiate a new beginning and an improved identity, while trying to remain true to themselves and their original background (Bowl, 2001).

Many mature students undertake higher education part-time. Externally generated differences play a determining role in the lifestyle choices and obligatory decisions of today's students. Due to domestic and financial obligations most mature students make the practical decision to study part-time to meet their other obligations. Reay (2002) observes that for many mature students lifestyle choices in higher education are dictated via external responsibilities in the form of domestic and employment responsibilities.

The *National Strategy for Higher Education to 2030* (HEA, 2011) reports that the needs of mature students can only be addressed through delivering of flexible learning opportunities, by way of part-time courses, flexibility within the delivery, work-based learning and the introduction of short intensive skills programmes.

Motivational factors, then, are varied, comprising personal development, altruism, human capital theory and economic rationalism. Many mature students are faced with multiple constraints in terms of finances and domestic responsibilities when deciding to enter higher education. Such constraints and motivational influencing factors need to be considered in terms of policy at national and institute level, so that mature students can be supported in a constructive way to ensure that the process of entering the field of higher education is truly equitable. The challenge in meeting the diverse needs of the mature student population requires provision of sound, rational advice within an integrated, inclusive service (Osborne et al., 2004).

# Part Two

Our trajectories

Ethnography and narratives became central to both our studies. We both acknowledge our personal areas of concern and interest as researchers. We cannot isolate ourselves from our studies. Ambreen presents her position from within a middle-class educated family, with a background of private schooling and her thought-provoking experiences in a government university. Teresa presents as a mature student during her educational trajectory. She is from a working-class background, the daughter of Irish emigrants, who aspired to hold a university degree similar to her participants in the study. Ambreen's research grew out of her experiences during teaching at the university in Sindh, whereas Teresa's research is based on her own life experiences that led her towards issues faced by mature students when they return to higher study.

It is interesting that as writers we share common goals and some common experiences in our quest to give voice to the unvoiced. We both positioned ourselves as 'in-between' researchers, meaning that while we, the 'in-between' researchers, are originally women sharing something common with our participants, we also understand the perspective of our academic Western readers. We are neither of the two alone. We have traces of both our participants and our readers in our lives. And therefore we are between our participants and our readers, helping to bridge the gap. In this part, we discuss our path through to this book and everything from our individual experiences in life and with different people, to our choice of research topic, all the way to publication.

*Chapter 3*

# How my journey through Pakistan began

*Ambreen Shahriar*

The biographical details of the researcher play a part in all qualitative research. They draw attention to the fact that the results are not objective, not absolute, but obtained by a specific researcher with specific life experiences (Woods, 1999). Qualitative writers prefer to write in the active rather than the passive voice (see Davies, 1982, cited in Woods, 1999). As my participants and my readers expect me to be aware of, and open about, my role in relation to my data, I write about my own background and experiences, and how these and my presence during the study might have affected my findings.

At the government university where I was studying for my undergraduate degree in English literature, a large number of the youngsters came from rural backgrounds. The mastery of written and spoken English was considered the greatest of a person's assets. I knew students who excelled in their L1 (either Sindhi or Urdu) literature class, which was compulsory during the first year of our undergraduate course, but who could not even be noticed by teachers in other classes, since English was the medium of instruction and in-class communication, and their own English was poor. One of my friends used to get top scores in her L1 class but not in the other subjects because of her inadequate command of English. At that time I didn't know what treasure went unexplored. None of our teachers ever bothered to ask those silent students or to encourage the diffident ones. They just regarded them as undeserving village bumpkins who had been badly educated. This negative attitude to such people is widespread (see, for example, Taylor, 1981). Later, when I joined the university as a lecturer, I tried to pay individual attention to such students, hoping to motivate them.

Once, however, a student in an undergraduate class of English literature really annoyed me. I asked him to come to the rostrum to repeat what I had explained to the class. He came forward confidently. He stood silently at the rostrum for minutes on end, at times smiling at his fellow students who were smiling back at him. But he couldn't utter a word. At first I felt sorry for him and gave him time. I asked him to say anything he wanted. Finally I asked him just to read from the book, but he couldn't even do that. I now wonder what went wrong with him; but more importantly how he would have been feeling about the whole incident. He came to the rostrum with such assurance, but he lost it when he was in front of a class of some 80 students, most of whom he knew well, and all of them encouraging him, as I could tell from their gestures. He was able to look at them, at their individual gestures and return smiles to them but ...

I thought and thought about the incident, then and now... The students all usually spoke quite happily, especially the men, whenever I asked them to. When a teacher looked at them, they felt important and their confidence was boosted. But after a while I began to understand that university teachers needed to know about the home culture of these students in order to make them better learners (see Obied, 2009). They had been brought up in an environment where children might have seen their fathers obeying the landlords and their mothers obeying their fathers. Everyone had a predefined role. Everybody had responsibilities. Nobody was allowed to speak, to express, to query or to question anything. Nobody: not their fathers, not their grandfathers, not their uncles, nobody; and definitely never ever women around them. Nobody had rights.

From early childhood, these undergraduate students might have experienced the severe consequences of expressing personal views or of arguing with a person in authority. They might have been doing manual work in their villages from the time they were little. They might have been beaten through no fault of their own by the *wadero* – the village landlord who pays *haris* to work in his fields. They might have been bullied because of their class. They could have been disgraced at any moment. And above all, they might have seen their fathers, helpless in the face of all this, being disgraced or beaten at any time. I recognized that it was this culture that they carried within themselves; culture that Sapir (1949: 197) defined as an 'impersonal aspect of those values and definitions which come to the child with the irresistible authority of father, mother, or other individuals', of which the child is only a 'passive recipient'. I thought and thought ... why they did not speak in class?, why was it that, when at last a teacher asked them to express themselves, some of them felt so good and became so happy, and spoke up, but others fell silent? I understood them all: students were not the same.

Recently a colleague of mine completed his doctorate in the UK. When he got the scholarship to study there, he said, 'Some people dream about achieving certain heights in their career and when they achieve them, they are very happy, but with my background, I never even *dreamt* of going to the UK.' He may have forgotten his words but they kept echoing in my mind.

Here is another example. It was the last class for a group of undergraduate students before their English literature exams. The students wanted to ask me questions related to the entire course. I invited a particular student to stand in front of the class and answer the questions of all the students. I was so confident about his subject knowledge and competence in English that I knew he would answer each question well. When I discussed my students in general and this session in particular with my colleagues in the staff room, I was astonished to learn from a colleague that she had taught this student during his first year at the university and that he had been one of those silent students who observe everything but never open their mouths. Later, when he obtained his Masters, he received a gold medal, and today he is an official in a private bank in Karachi. This goes to show how much these suppressed children can achieve given half a chance.

So many incidents and so many people around me – students and friends – left me thinking. I began to understand that these people with their humble backgrounds have a lot of experience of life to share. I decided to collect life stories of students from poor rural backgrounds for my research. At first I intended to conduct a comparative study on participants who have completed their education and are on a sound career path and those who quit university a month or so after joining (Shahriar, 2012, 2013a). After an initial study, however, this differentiation into success vs. failure did not seem so relevant. I realized that it was not only their academic success that was important but their entire lives. Every detail, every small incident helped to make them the people they are. Therefore, I widened my objective into simply gathering and interpreting the life stories of young Sindhis from poor rural backgrounds who aspired to a better life, and for whom higher education was their source of empowerment.

## Theory in research

With my educational background of English literature and TESOL, it was not easy to choose a theory for this study that is completely related to the sociology of education. However, I finally came across Bourdieu, and adopted his theory as my framework for this study (see Shahriar, 2015).

One reason I use Bourdieu's theoretical framework is that he discusses the power relations existing in any force field so helpfully (as presented in Figure 3.1 below). He explains class divisions in terms that go beyond economic differences, which holds true for Sindhi society. He describes how all agents, dominant and dominated, actively participate in the power struggles inherent in the social order. Each agent receives a *habitus* – that is, code of practice – from the force field and in turn changes the force field. Consequently, according to Bourdieu, individual agents have the ability to transform their lives, challenge the existing systems, develop a subversive habitus, use reflexivity – the tendency to interpret and act according to personal judgement.

The balance between structure and agency that Bourdieu created through the concept of habitus is convincing, and it seems to work in the case of my participants. Clearly the bigger social world is decisive in making my participants what they are today. Against all these forces, my participants try to transform their habitus by making difficult choices that are rare in their environment. Such choices do exist but are seldom exercised.

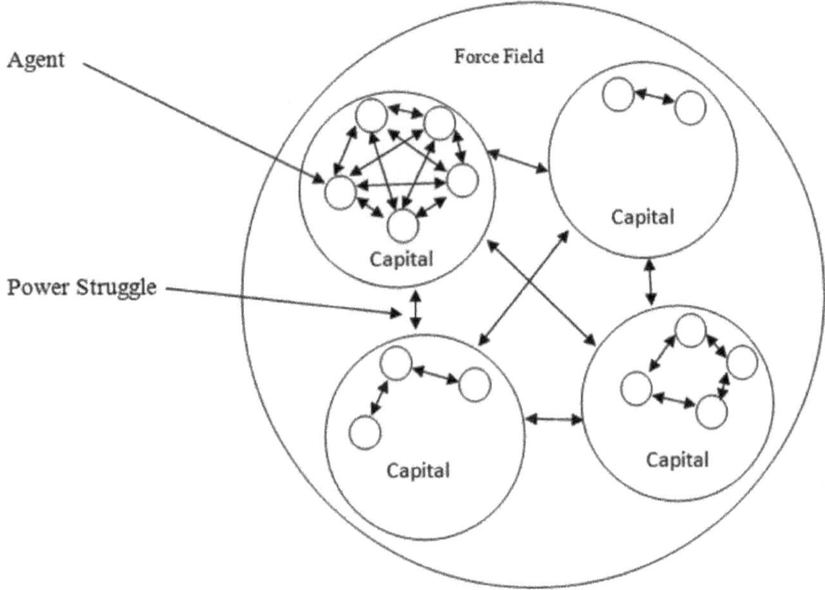


**Figure 3.1:** Power Struggle in Force Field

## Once in the field

I encountered several problems in the field, of which some were social and cultural, and others intellectual. People did not want to wash their dirty linen in public, they were not prepared to make their and their family's shortcomings known. That's why they were reluctant to give a life story interview. Two girls refused to be interviewed because their elder brother did not want them to. One young man kept assuring me that he would come, but did not turn up. The people on my list bailed out one by one, giving various reasons: that they could not spare even one hour (not credible), or assuring me of their willingness to participate and then not turning up. I was most surprised by two female colleagues at the university where I worked as Associate Professor, who declined to be interviewed because I would be recording their voices. Alasuutari (1995: 52) tells us 'that if the researcher makes friends with the informants, and the informants trust the researcher, they will also be honest with the researcher.' The reverse is also true: without trust I cannot obtain reliable data. From this experience I learnt that similar, and maybe more complex, problems await me in the field. I also learnt how careful I would have to be when talking to my participants about their actions – if at all – and how important it was not to upset them or inhibit them by making comments that might appear to be judgmental (Hammersley, 1994).

The disastrous floods in Pakistan in August 2010 prevented me from travelling to visit most of my participants, so I had largely to rely on them to come to me. I refunded their travel costs, which most of them refused to accept; however, I gave them presents as a token of my appreciation. But my gestures were greatly outweighed by the efforts some made to enable my study to succeed. Abdur Razzak came from a flooded area and attended even though his father had died only a few days earlier. Shabana had come to my city to attend a workshop. She knew she had to travel for several hours the next morning, yet she agreed to give the interview in the evening, after her workshop was over. I conducted Farhana's interview late at night, at around 11.00 p.m., because that was the only time we both had available. So even though some people did not turn up and others dropped out at the last minute, others made an enormous effort to get their voices heard by the world. One might argue that there was some principle of 'natural selection' at work here, and that those people who made it through to the interviews in spite of all obstacles were exactly the people I wanted, who would serve my purposes best. That is why I believe that we must not wait for the most suitable time, the best – most willing and enthusiastic – people will turn out at the most difficult times.

A few interesting incidents occurred during data collection. I describe some in the following section on reflexivity.

## Reflexivity

Research in the social world is affected by the physical presence of the researcher (Bourdieu, 1977; Clifford and Marcus, 1986; Kenway and McLeod, 2004). Believing in complete objectivity is to deny the presence of the researcher herself and the research participants and deny the identities and individualities of all those involved in the research. However, research on human subjects cannot be completely subjective either. Adopting a completely subjective approach would be to ignore the objective realities like race, colour, language, social status, chance happenings and so on, all of which are beyond the will and effort of human agents.

The question of power relations (Miller and Glassner, 2004) is also applicable. Edwards and Talbot (1994: 14) advise that while collecting data, the researcher must always ask herself, 'am I taking undue advantage of my position to gain information?' Although I was not doing so deliberately, it seems to me that I have an undue advantage because of my position as a university teacher in Pakistan, a researcher and above all a PhD student from the UK. My position as an interviewer was one of authority. I was motivated by the desire to find out as much as possible about the lives of my participants but I must admit that presumably they agreed to be interviewed more out of respect for me than because they wished to *give* as much information as possible about their lives. I used phenomenographic interviews (see Marton, 1981, cited in Francis, 1993) to compensate for the problems of power relations.

## Issues of translation

Denzin (1991: 68, cited in Miller and Glassner, 2004) notes:

> The subject [participant] is more than can be contained in a text, and the text is only a reproduction of what the subject has told us. What the subject tells us is itself something that has been shaped by prior cultural understandings. Most important, language, which is our window into the subject's world (and our world), plays tricks. It displaces the very thing it is supposed to represent, so that what is always given is a trace of other things, not the thing – lived experience – itself.

Miller and Glassner (2004: 134) note that a researcher's tool for rebuilding and understanding reality is the language the interviewee uses. It can only rebuild a part of reality. To this they add that 'the language of interviewing fractures the stories being told' and that the process of 'the research commits further fractures as well'. Language is of special significance in my research, as it is conducted in a context very different from that in which it is going to be read. With such deep cultural differences between my participants and my readers, the responsibility lies with me to convey through this piece the essence of this research. That is, I therefore discuss the issues related to translation and interpretation in some detail here.

My research is based at a public university, the University of Sindh, with students of varying social and educational backgrounds. The language of informal communication at the university is Sindhi. But the language of education and learning is English. Urdu is used when one of the parties in any informal communication is a L1 Urdu speaker. I conducted the interviews in Sindhi, which is my mother tongue and that of the participants. This was a natural thing to do in a situation where all the participants have the same mother tongue and where needlessly using another language would inevitably impede communication. However, for the sake of research and publication, the words of my participants had to be translated into, or reported in, English. While translating, interpreting and analysing the data, I was seriously worried lest my final text should lose the flavour of the original. I refer here to the Italian dictum: *traduttore, traditore* (Thou art a traitor, translator).

Following Catford (1965), Bassnett (2002) recognizes two types of untranslatability:

- linguistic untranslatability, when the target language lacks a syntactic or lexical equivalent for a feature or item of the source language, and
- cultural untranslatability, when the target culture lacks an equivalent for a situational feature in the source culture. While translating and interpreting my data, I encountered both types of untranslatability.

## Linguistic untranslatability

- 'Then my father stopped working and, as they say, even when you have tons of rations to feed yourself on, if you are not earning anymore, the same tons of ration may end before you realise.' (Abdur Razzak)
- 'Till the truth is revealed, lies eat up a person' means, until the truth is known, lies will mentally disturb and eventually destroy a person. (Shabana)
- 'My parents [are aged], my brothers were young, who would take out the thorns,' meaning, 'who would help them in their time of adversity'. (Shabana)
- 'My brother's home was being destroyed' actually means 'his life', but we use the word *ghar* (home) for the life a man spends with his wife and children, as also in another common expression is make one's own home, which means 'get married'. (Shabana)

## Cultural untranslatability

- Ahmar told me how his mother used to prepare him and his brother for school by oiling their hair before combing it, and putting *surmo* on their eyelashes and around the contours of their eyes. *Surmo* is a cosmetic like kohl, a black powder that is applied with a thin metallic rod called *sarai*. The effect is similar, but not identical, to mascara and eyeliner. *Surmo* is banned in the UK for health reasons; the word and the use of the substance are not known to the 'non-Asian' population of the UK.
- The word *kacho* used by Abdur Razzak can be translated as 'rural area', but no exact equivalent is available in English since *kacho* refers to an area where there are ditches, dunes and swamps, unclean water, open drains or no drainage – an unsanitary area.
- In Farhana's interview I didn't know how to translate the Sindhi word *mathan*, which means 'above'. She is talking about examiners being sent by higher authorities, so we just say 'they are sent from above'. This could have a religious connotation in that prophets are sent from God and God 'lives in the sky above'. So the authority, or people in authority are always referred to as 'above'.
- 'Given water on the charpoy' is a phrase that means a lazy bum, usually a man, who spends all day lying on a Pakistani-style camp-bed, *Khatta* in Sindhi, doesn't work, is useless in the household, is given iced-drinks and served left, right and centre by the hard-working womenfolk in his household. He is something akin to, but not identical to the couch potato Onslow in the BBC TV series *Keeping Up Appearances*, 1990 and 1995. (Farwa)

Bakhtin (1981) advises that, when translating, the translator should always carefully consider the context. From the meaning of the word to its speaker to the significance of the event it is used to express, everything is determined by the context:

- the time and place of the utterance
- the listeners
- the social status of both the speaker and the listener
- the power relationship
- the significance of the incident for the speaker and also for the listener.

Accordingly, I advise my readers to keep the context in mind while reading my work. My participants, both male and female, talk about how they, or others around them, sometimes got a good hiding or were slapped by parents and teachers. This is common in our culture, as we believe that corporal punishment is effective, not necessarily harmful and not in itself unjust if a child has overstepped the mark.

Hazrat Ali, the Prophet's cousin and son-in-law, first Muslim child and later a great Muslim scholar, said: 'When a parent beats the child, it is like putting manure on a young crop'. People of all Muslim denominations respect and accept his religious knowledge. The Prophet Muhammad himself, however, is reported in one of the *hadiths* – the recorded sayings – to have said: 'Do not lift your stick against your wife and children and urge them to fear Allah, The Almighty.' This shows that questions of corporal punishment are in flux in Islam, as they are in Christendom. Even in England, two sayings with roots in the Bible contradict contemporary legislation:

> Spare the rod, and spoil the child' based on 'He that spareth his rod hateth his son: but he that loveth him chasteneth him betimes. (Old Testament: Proverbs 13:24)
>
> For whom the Lord loveth he chasteneth, and scourgeth every son whom he receiveth. (New Testament: Hebrews 12:6, King James translation; an alternative translation would be: 'because the Lord disciplines the one he loves, and he chastens everyone he accepts as his son')

Since parents and teachers are jointly responsible for developing a child's healthy personality, in our culture they have a right to chastise the child for their own good. None of my participants is ashamed of talking about this, as they realize that almost everyone had the same experiences when they were young. None of them resents the elders who administered such punishments. Punishing children when they deserve it is also a religious duty. I see it as an important Eastern value.

Returning to common expressions, all the participants, especially Abdur Razzak and Farhana, used Arabic expressions such as *Inshallah* (meaning 'God willing', 'If God wills'), *Mashallah* (meaning 'Hallelujah' = Praise the Lord) and *Alhamdulillah* (meaning 'Thank God') every now and then when talking about such chastisements.

Using such expressions is common for Muslims across the world, whatever their native language. None of my participants can speak Arabic apart from such common words and phrases. People from the Indian subcontinent recite the Qur'an in Arabic but they read it translated into their mother tongue so that they can understand it. Shabana talks about remembering Allah, reciting the Qur'an, prayer and *tasbeeh* (repeatedly reciting prayer using a rosary with 100 beads), when times were hard for her family. *Tasbeeh* is similar to Mantra Jaap (chanting Mantra using *mala*, a rosary with 108 beads) in Hinduism, or Roman Catholics saying the rosary, as well as similar practices in other religions.

There were also some peculiar, personal tags. For example, Farwa used the expression *Keena budhayan* every now and then. This means 'how should I tell you'. It does not mean that she is unable to explain something; she was just saying it out of habit, to gain time to think and to keep the channel of communication open. Many people use this or other such phrases for maintaining a conversation in Sindhi. Similar expressions exist in other languages, for example in English: 'How shall I put it?', as in E.M. Forster's *Howards End* (1973: 180), where Margaret says with shy hesitation to her newly acquired fiancé Henry: 'On the stage, or in books, a proposal is – how shall I put it? – a full-blown affair, a kind of bouquet; it loses its literal meaning.'

There were many such cases when translating, and explaining was difficult since 'all translation is only a somewhat provisional way of coming to terms with the foreignness of languages' (Benjamin, 1969: 75, cited in Ding, 2008). I did what I could by providing a fairly literal translation and then explaining it to my Western readers.

*Chapter 4*

# How my own journey began

*Teresa Bruen*

> *There is no end to education. It is not that you read a book, pass an examination, and finish with education. The whole of life, from the moment you are born to the moment you die, is a process of learning.*
>
> Jiddu Krishnamurti

My own educational trajectory was the overriding reason for my research and the path it followed. Many personal experiences have contributed to my professional identity overall, and here I discuss how greatly they influenced my decisions about the research and the methods I employed. As my research followed the path of narrative, I believe it to be important that my narrative, too, is visible. Consequently my chapters in the book highlight my personal path, give direction to the research and demonstrate how, in the realm of qualitative research, the personal threads through the professional.

I am a child of Irish immigrants who found themselves as economic migrants in Birmingham, England, in the late 1950s. My mother and father came from small farming backgrounds in rural areas of the West of Ireland, and had very little money. Devout Catholics, they came from large families. The importance of education was not greatly emphasized.

This characterized all economically disadvantaged families in Ireland at the time. Only the wealthy were given the opportunity to attend full secondary-level schooling and move on to higher education. The cost of education was prohibitive; my parents came from families who had no history nor culture of nurturing education. Education wasn't viewed as a valuable commodity so was not part of their families' everyday culture. In this they were no different from their community. However, their life experiences and their missed opportunities affected the way they regarded education and this in turn influenced my educational trajectory.

My mother left school at 14 years of age and worked as a housekeeper for a priest in her local village. She had a love of the Irish language and wanted to complete her secondary education but economic constraints prevented her. She handed over the money she earned to her parents to help with the cost of feeding and clothing her siblings. At the age of 17 she migrated to England, settling in Birmingham. She stayed in the local YWCA and procured employment in a nearby factory. To this day she tells the story about how for the first week she had no money for lunch. The women she worked with noticed that she didn't eat at lunchtime and offered to share their lunch with her, but she was too proud and refused, pretending she wasn't hungry.

My father also migrated to England at 17 years of age. He would have attended secondary school up until that point and was educated in a monastery. He thought he had a vocation to become religious, which meant his schooling would have been free. He met my mother and they married and had three children: two boys and me.

Religion played a very important part in our family home. We were raised as practising Catholics, and I attended a Catholic girls' school managed by the order of the Sisters of Mercy. The family moved back to Ireland in the late 1970s and I finished my secondary-level education in a convent school for girls, again managed by the religious order of the Sisters of Mercy.

My mother was a guiding influence all through my school years. She placed huge importance on the value of obtaining a good education, especially for girls. She believed that education ensured that a woman would be financially independent and have a fulfilling, exciting life. So I grew up believing that education was important and that it was valued in my family home. After I sat the Leaving Certificate, I chose to undertake a career in nursing and was accepted to study in a nursing school in north London. Nursing education at that time was delivered within specialist nursing schools in partnership with clinical learning environments in hospital settings. It was therefore was separate from third-level institutions.

The qualification awarded after a three-year period of study and clinical practice was at the level of professional certificate. I practised as a general nurse in various clinical settings for years, gaining vast experience. After several years I chose to return to Ireland, where I studied in a midwifery school and qualified as a midwife.

I became interested in working in the community setting, and so I undertook a Higher Diploma in Public Health Nursing. Once qualified, I began work in the West of Ireland as a public health nurse and had a relatively large and varied caseload. I enjoyed the variety of the work, delivering health promotion programmes, caring for the elderly, engaging in child developmental work and teaching students who came to me on placement.

While I was working in the field of public health, the profession of nursing entered the domain of third-level institutes and a bachelor of science honours degree in nursing was developed. I decided to return to education as a mature student, to take this degree, possibly influenced by my mother's strong belief in the importance of education for women, but also because I realized that the members of the interdisciplinary team I worked with had all been educated to honours degree level. I believed there was a certain credibility that I, as merely a certificate trained nurse, lacked. I felt professionally on the back foot, unable to hold my own. But I welcomed the fact that nursing was to be delivered in institutes of higher education at honours degree level.

So when the bachelor of science honours degree became available, I decided to apply. Two significant factors helped me to make this decision. Firstly, the degree was offered on a part-time basis in a university that was geographically accessible – a three-hour round trip drive away. Secondly, the Health Board I was working for allowed me the time off to attend and, as part of continual professional development, they agreed to pay 50 per cent of my fees on successful completion. Thirdly, my mother agreed to come to my home one day a week to care for my young children. Although I mention this last, it really was the most significant factor in my taking on the university course. My life was made so much easier at every level by her commitment to my children and to me and my education. By her actions she demonstrated in a superbly practical fashion how important she believed education to be. I've never underestimated the gift she gave me of attending university, safe in the knowledge that my children were being well cared for within their own home.

As I reflect on this period of my life, I appreciate that this was life defining for me at both a professional and a personal level. I cannot stress enough that this was really the start of my educational journey. That opportunity, the geographical location, the time granted for me to attend plus the financial aid started me on a lifelong journey and enabled me to become the first member of my family to attend and succeed at university and ultimately fulfil my ambition to work within the field of higher education.

I continued my professional and academic career and engaged in higher education through programmes that were delivered on a part-time basis, were geographically accessible and, importantly, suited my family and employment commitments. I was the mature student, trying to juggle work, finance, study and family commitments, determined to succeed, wanting to lead the way for my own family and to follow my mother's advice.

## The present

I've had the good fortune to be employed as a lecturer in a third-level institute in the West of Ireland for the past 14 years. The West of Ireland,

and specifically the province of Connaught, has a magnificent scenic coastline along the Atlantic Ocean. The counties of Mayo, Sligo, Leitrim, Galway and Roscommon make up Connaught, the least inhabited province in Ireland, with a population of just over 400,000.

The HEI I'm employed in is situated in a small rural market town. The institute opened its doors in 1994, housed in a sensitively restored old hospital building, retaining much of the architectural grandeur while delivering modern, up-to-date facilities for the student body. It serves the needs of the local community and the environs while also attracting people from other areas of Ireland. In its mission statement, the institute 'aims to develop life-long learning opportunities through our teaching and research, by supporting regional development consistent with national higher education policy.'

I think it is important for the reader to have a sense of the setting where the research took place and the area where the students lived and studied. The town itself – it is not a city – is small and condensed and has little industry. Driving into it, one is aware of the beauty of the countryside, the greenness of the fields and the sense of nature, stillness and quiet. Of course this goes hand in hand with a rural area of small farms on poor, rugged land.

I drive a 70-km round trip every day to work and I feel blessed as I enjoy the peace and quiet, admiring the beautiful scenery before spending my days indoors teaching. But we reside in a province of which it was said during the famine years 'To Hell or to Connaught'. This reflects how poor and unmanageable the farmland was – and remains still. Farmers cannot make a living from their land in this mainly agricultural area, so they are subsidized by the EU, and many farmers also work in other employment to support their farming lifestyle and hold onto their land. Historically, the Irish people have a special passion about owning their land ever since their oppression by English landlords and colonialists, and do not forget the wars that were fought to own the land in their own right.

While working at the institute, I became involved, along with other interested academics and relevant stakeholders from the field of social care practice, in the development of the curriculum for the BA in applied social care. I had worked for ten years in the community setting, bringing expertise and knowledge to the task, and was immensely excited about the project.

The field of social care practice within Ireland had, prior to this, been relatively unregulated. However, CORU, Ireland's multi-professional health regulator, which was established under the Health and Social Care

Professionals Act 2005, is now in place. Its role is fundamentally and significantly to protect the public through the preferment of high standards of professional conduct, education, training and competence through the statutory regulation of health and social care professionals. This requires social care workers who had previously been working in the field of social care practice to undertake a third-level qualification in order to register with CORU to continue their practice.

This requirement, along with student demand within the area, was the impetus for the development of the programme. Like other academics in the field, and because of my practical experience, I was interested in the suggested philosophy of the programme, which incorporates the principles of justice, equality and fairness. It fosters an approach to learning that facilitates and encourages the students' self-development and has a student-centred approach to learning. I lectured on the programme on areas of health promotion, community development and care in the community setting. Reflecting on my own trajectory as a mature student, I see that it was this philosophy of equality and justice that steered me towards my research enquiry.

In approaching the enquiry, it was important to reflect also on my own world view as shaped by my experiences as a mature student. I am aware that personal experiences, culture and history may shape the paradigm formed by the researcher. I was conscious and ever-mindful that my background and learning helped inform my choices of methodology (Creswell, 2007). Indeed I was cognisant of the notion of the naivety of the researcher undertaking qualitative enquiry who believes that they can report their findings without their own ideas or notions becoming part of it.

My experiences of working with the first cohort of applied social studies students further motivated me to undertake this research enquiry. Over a third of the 40-student cohort were mature students. They brought to the educational space their personal life experiences, which they shared willingly with the class when we discussed the issues of social inequality, and the pursuit of a fair and just system for all. Many of the mature students spoke about their experiences of their trajectory through primary and second-level schools and their journey towards the field of higher education. I became deeply interested in their stories and the manner in which they told them. They showed no rancour about an educational system that had treated them so unfairly but were accepting of their lot, normalizing their situations through exchanging and comparing their stories, amid lots of laughter and some tears too.

Their stories were shocking and saddening, but always uplifting because they were so proud of their current achievements. They were truly embracing their student status. They presented differently from the traditional student who comes straight into the field of higher education from secondary school. The mature students appeared amazed that anyone would be interested in listening to their stories, and this is apparent in the research. It shows the effects of years of oppression within educational institutes that did not value their voice because of their culture and socio-economic background. Reay (2002: 407) has identified such students as having 'a troubled educational history'.

The students' sharing of their experiences became the lifeblood of the classroom and the discussions. They told me that they gathered in their houses and the learning went on long after the lectures had finished. Such passion for learning from people who had previously been marginalized and isolated within their schooling fascinated me. They seemed to blossom before my eyes. They were growing in self-worth, their experiences were being valued and they were surviving a culture that had essentially dismissed them, albeit in a subtle but precise and effective way. So what was different for them now? This question was the genesis for my research.

The undergraduate programme, its philosophy and content, appeared to enable and encourage these students' voices. It was the ideal space for them. They discovered the freedom to express themselves in a safe environment, and did so through telling stories, spontaneously adopting a qualitative narrative approach. Irish people have a history of story-telling – it's a tradition within our communities. A story-teller in times gone by was called a *seanchai* and was generally a man who went from house to house and had the gift of keeping his audience enraptured by the stories he told. He was highly valued and respected. The tradition of story-teller persists in Ireland, in the guise of comedians, poets and playwrights. My decision to employ a narrative approach was ontologically and philosophically influenced in that it places the person at the heart of the enquiry and signals the importance of their stories, paying particular attention to individual experience. Stories give people a platform to talk freely about the things that are important to them.

## Searching for theory

Next I had to consider how I would analyse the students' stories. Choosing a narrative methodology was the easy part – a natural choice. But how to analyse their stories? What conceptual framework would help me to capture the stories, to explain them fully in all their multilayered richness? This was of the utmost importance: I didn't want to overlook or misinterpret their stories of such significance. I didn't want to rob the students of their voice. If they were willing to share their stories with me, my responsibility was to present their voices to the world in a meaningful, honest and authentic manner. I had to endeavour to make sense of the stories so I could explain their significance to the field of education.

Searching for a theory that is the correct fit can be a troublesome and lengthy process but this turned out not to be the case here. During my doctoral studies I had the good fortune to be introduced to the theories of French sociologist Pierre Bourdieu and was immediately drawn to his work. It made sense that this was the framework I would employ. Bourdieu examines the social struggle that is the field of education. Through his conceptual framework of field, habitus and capital, he illuminates the varying, sometimes subtle, power struggles and the oppression of certain elements of society within the field of education. Bourdieu's work focuses on the issues of social inequality and justice, especially in relation to education. Bourdieu dedicated himself to the analysis of education throughout his academic career, and I believed that his theoretical framework would be an ideal prism through which to examine the experiences of the mature students in my study.

What I find particularly useful is how Bourdieu seeks to explore below the surface, investigating and examining how social systems work (Mills and Gale, 2007). He demonstrates a wonderful understanding of the arena of education, proposing that it was a field that reproduced itself more than others do. This I find hugely significant. How do we improve if we are perpetually reproducing and reinforcing the same inequalities? The first step must surely be to acknowledge that this pattern exists and bring it into the light for examination.

Bourdieu noted that social agents who were in dominant positions within education tended to be entrenched within its practices and discourse (Bourdieu and Passeron, 1990). Much of his research focuses on the area of social struggle, examining those who are sidelined and how they manage within that space of marginalization (Bourdieu, 1990). He investigates social differentiation, class reproduction and hierarchies of power within the education system (Grenfell, 2004). And he further proposes that those involved in the education system reproduce the social order, not realizing that they are part of the process and therefore part of the overall problem.

I see Bourdieu as a critical social theorist who is interested in social struggle and who exposes and illuminates social inequalities so that they can be understood in a way that can ultimately lead to change. Accordingly,

I use Bourdieu's theory of practice and his key and interrelated concepts of habitus, field and capital as a lens through which to explore the experiences of the mature students.

## Being present in the field

The concept of the field was useful to me throughout my enquiry. It allowed me to focus on the site of education at both a local level – the institute where I was working and conducted the enquiry – and also at a national and global level. The mature students were enthusiastic about telling their stories. There were, however, challenges while working in the field. Although the students were fervent about telling and sharing their narratives, finding time to meet was a difficulty. All had caring commitments such as dependent children or elderly parents who consumed a great deal of their time. Therefore a lot of flexibility and creativity was needed. Meetings had to happen at a time and place that suited them and sometimes meetings had to be cut short only to resume at a later date. This highlighted their commitment to the research and to having their voices heard.

I remained as a full-time lecturer, working within the constraints of a full teaching load. I could not cancel classes and I had numerous other roles and responsibilities within the institute. In addition, there were the family commitments, children at an important stage in their own education, facing life-defining examinations, so requiring my support and advice as well as the usual care and sustenance. All these challenges were overcome with hard work, determination and motivation to get the work completed.

The time that gathering the narratives took presented challenges, too. There is no way to decide how long someone's story will take. How many hours do you put aside to hear a person's story? Managing the interview process, listening to the significant parts of their account, gently guiding the student to express and focus on the weighty issues of their narrative is a complex process. It requires skill, subtlety and consideration to ensure that important areas are not overlooked.

On reflection, however, I saw that my own situation tallied with parts of the narratives of the students. The complexities of life, the choices we make, the sacrifices that allow us to pursue academic success and fulfilment, to reach our potential, were all experiences we had in common.

## Reflexivity and positionality of the researcher

The contention is that the researcher cannot be totally objective or detached from the knowledge they are generating and therefore should aim to understand their role in the overall process. Consequently during the course of this enquiry, I was conscious of the importance of reflecting upon my own narrative and how this would impact upon the research. I became aware of the concepts of personal and social justification and the importance of addressing both these notions. Accordingly I had to consider the justification for my enquiry in relation to my own interests, and also its potential benefits to the mature student population, into whom I believed I had especially relevant personal insight.

It has been observed that asking oneself difficult questions is an integral part of reflexivity; I found this a useful concept that guided me throughout the research process. The power within an interview situation generally lies with the interviewer. They direct the flow of the interview and choose any quotes to be used. There is always an asymmetry within the relationship that must be acknowledged and explored throughout. Awareness may be sufficient to balance the challenges of the interview process.

# Part Three

Giving voice to the unheard

In this part we invite our readers to listen to the voices and views of our sample: all of them people who have not been given the chance in their lives to speak up for themselves. As Teresa argues, the voice of the mature students is their new-found strength: likewise poverty, sociocultural and economic pressures kept Ambreen's participants quiet so as not to disturb the status quo. We collected the interviews in the participants' first languages (L1). Translating Ambreen's interviews from Sindhi verbatim to allow the voices of the men and women to be heard is one of the central aims of her chapter. Teresa places the voices of her participants at the forefront of her research while wrapping their narratives in a cloak of context that acknowledges multivoicedness through narrative enquiry. The stories her participants presented she considers to be reflections of and reactions to their experiences of life.

Teresa constructed her chapter according to the emerging themes – to provide a sharp and explicit focus on her mature students' experiences – the central aim of her study. Ambreen presents the stories of the pain that motivates her participants to struggle. However, the purpose of using narrative is not only to collect honest, true-life stories, but also to see what the participants want others to see and understand about how they view the world. Therefore, whatever we two researchers gathered gave us enough to understand the world in which our participants live and the way they perceive how this world responds to them, and this is why we can bring our readers such insight into lives so different from our own.

*Chapter 5*

# Making a better life: The voices from rural Sindh

*Ambreen Shahriar*

Social science research explores the perceptions of social actors (Miller and Glassner, 2004; Charmaz, 1995). My study tries to understand the meaning my participants attribute to the events and incidents in their lives; I want to understand the way they see the world they live in. I focus on the uniqueness of my participants and their situations, and that is why I follow an ethnographic approach. Its suitability for research on human behaviour is widely accepted (Bruyn, 1966; Blumer, 1969; Harré and Secord, 1973 – all cited in Hammersley, 1994). It can give us a profound understanding of behaviour, of the complexity of relations and everyday life, of power relations, of many significant trivialities that seem so insignificant that they are hardly ever noticed. My study is indeed ethnographic in nature because:

- Its participants have a common culture or world view (Alasuutari, 1998; Hammersley, 1994)
- It seeks to understand human behaviour from the participant's point of view (Fetterman, 1998; Clifford, 1988; Kamil et al., 1985)
- It identifies and describes phenomena from beginning to end across cycles (Edwards and Talbot, 1994; Kamil et al., 1985)
- It develops hypotheses grounded in the event and driven by the conceptual framework of the study (Hammersley, 1994; Kamil et al., 1985)
- It presents a vivid picture of another culture to its readers (Alasuutari, 1998; Geertz, 1988)
- It provides emic – insider's or native's – perspective (Robson, 2002; Fetterman, 1998; Hammersley, 1994; Nader, 1993).

It can be called 'a study of multiple cases', or 'a case study that is ethnographic in nature'. Feagin et al. (1991: 9) regard case study as a holistic approach and note that it 'can permit the researcher to examine not only the complex life in which people are implicated but also the impact on beliefs and decisions of the complex web of social interaction'. Case study is advantageous for my research field, as it can provide fundamental insights, detailed analysis and rich and in-depth description (Feagin et al., 1991; Sjoberg et al., 1991). Mine is a 'descriptive multiple-case study' (Yin, 2003: 5).

My research tool for this study was life stories. An important reason behind choosing life stories as a research method is that narrative 'is international, trans-historical, trans-cultural: it is simply there, like life itself' (Barthes, 1977: 79). Telling and listening to stories is common in everyday life across cultures. The translatability of narrative is accepted by Barthes (1977), Lejeune (1989), Mishler (1986), Rosen (1998) and White (1981). Through in-depth life story interviews I learnt about the views and ideas of my participants and give voice to them. I have tried to present reality as seen by the interviewees 'with depth and detail' (Bourdieu et al., 1999; Fowler, 1996). This sociocultural perspective of reality has great significance for my participants, and for me and the social world where this reality belongs.

Before going into the field, I decided that, as a matter of principle, I would only interview people who were happy to tell their stories. Therefore the main criterion for choosing participants became whether or not they wanted their voices to be heard. I found two men and three women who came from poor and restrictive backgrounds and were trying to find a way through higher education to escape from their poverty. All my participants belong to various villages of the province of Sindh. Their families are of varying socio-economic status, though all come from families that suffer considerable economic hardship. And the same is true for the extent of education in each family, in the case of their parents and siblings. All of them, however, speak Sindhi as L1 – their first language. These are the five people who struggled through their lives and some still struggle, but importantly, they are proud of their efforts and have no intention of giving up in the face of adversity. Each was happy and excited to share their experiences of life.

I would like to arrange these five strong-minded people in the order of professional success each is now enjoying:

- Ahmar is an officer in the Pakistan Air Force; he has completed his journey of struggle and it is his time for enjoying its yield
- Farwa is an assistant professor in a university; she has reached a good status professionally and is currently doing a PhD

- Shabana completed her Masters in Chemistry, has been working in NGOs and is currently doing an internship but she does not yet have a permanent job, therefore her struggle goes on
- Farhana is currently not in work despite completing her undergraduate course in one field, changing to another for postgraduate study, keeping in mind the job market, and enjoying a government job for more than four years
- Abdur Razzak, who quit university a month after joining for his undergrad degree owing to family circumstances, resumed his job as a clerk at a school. He is now struggling to take a degree in law so that he can make a career in that field.

## Patterns that connect

Kearney (1998: 310) argues that 'to some extent in the modern world, we are all exiles. We are all living in translations.' The stories narrated by my five participants show the continuous state of translation they are in (Shahriar, 2013a). This chapter is based on the underlying patterns evident in the overall stories of my participants that connect them with each other and with all those who have strength to struggle against the odds (see also Shahriar, 2013b). These patterns can be placed in three layers – self, family and society – but the layers are so confusingly overlapping and intermingled that separating incidents and putting them under each heading is impossible. My participants live with many people around them: their important others include those in their immediate families, in their extended families, in their neighbourhoods, in their schools, in their friends' circles, in their villages, and each of them leaves a mark on their lives.

## Self

> *One cannot cross the sea merely by standing and staring at the water*
>
> Rabindranath Tagore

My participants took courage and followed their hearts' desire. As Abdur Razzak says, 'everyone makes his life on his own, either he makes it a hell or heaven, it depends on oneself.' This attitude is summed up by the Latin proverb: '*Sui quisque fortunae faber est*' ('Everybody is the maker of his own fortune') and also by Goethe's 1777 poem '*Beherzigung*' (Encouragement), which is remarkably apt for my participants and their determination (see Figure 5.1).

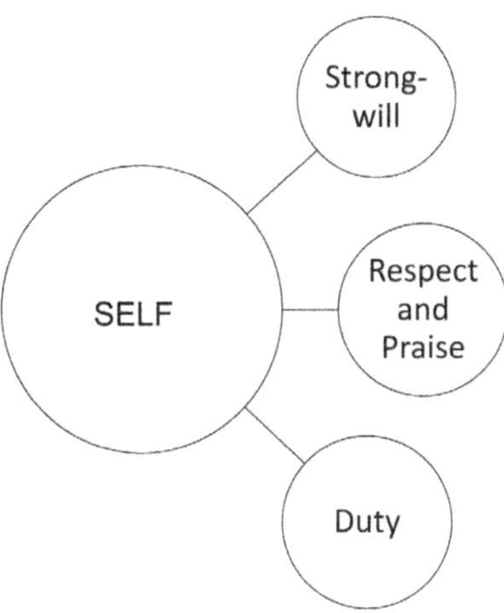


**Figure 5.1:** Self

## *Strong will*

Of all five participants, Shabana was the most resolute. When she passed her final exams at secondary school, her father decided to send her to university, in spite of neighbours' tongues wagging. He insisted, 'My daughter will go to university. Who cares if I am a Hafiz! [Hafiz mean a person who learns the Qur'an by heart; such people are highly respected among the people around and are given high ranks in religion.] My daughter is entitled to study. It is her right. We will not prevent her from being educated just because she is a girl. To me she is a son.' It was at about that time that Shabana learnt that she was married. Her grandfather had wanted to develop a close bond between his sons (Shabana's father and her uncle) in his life. He therefore had five-day-old Shabana married to her four-day-old cousin. He also got Shabana's elder brother (a step-brother) married to her cousin (sister of her husband). Child marriage in order to form alliances and protect family property was equally common in feudal families in medieval Europe.[1]

However, Shabana and her family were humiliated by her in-laws for being parents of a daughter and for being poor, to keep them submissive and grateful in the same way as poor little Fanny in Jane Austen's *Mansfield Park* (1814). They tried to restrict Shabana's movements, her education and did what they could to make her and her family's lives a misery. When Shabana was in her final year at university, her in-laws filed a court case against her father for not allowing Shabana to move to her husband's home. Shabana says: 'I was young and still living with my parents; but I was old enough to make decisions. I looked through the attitudes of people around me.' She was in the grip of – and battling against – class-ridden, gender-ridden present-day Pakistani society, in which only might is right. Only men or the rich have power, but despite being neither, Shabana refused to accept herself as weak.

When her in-laws filed their court case to force her to join her husband, she filed for a divorce. It was all-out war now. Her family, especially her mother, was not happy with her decision because stigma is attached to a divorced woman, even if she had cause to initiate the divorce. People in our society think that there must be something wrong with her. 'Please do not dishonour our family by insisting on this divorce,' her mother wailed. 'You are a daughter, it does not matter if *your* life is destroyed.' Shabana argued back:

> Listen, Mother, when you were young, you listened to your brothers and married a man who was three times your age. ... Did they think of *your* happiness? How did *you* benefit by following that advice? For whom did you sacrifice your youth and your life? Why did you sacrifice your life? What good has it done you? ... What did I learn from you, I should also do the same thing then what would the future hold? Nothing at all. So I would have to face the situation, else nothing will change ever.

So many questions! And Shabana could not think of any answer but rebellion, rebellion against the standard social norms.

Another male participant, Ahmar, was troubled by the quarrels at the village during his stay at the hostel at the University of Sindh and during his entire university life. He always asked his father not to quarrel with others and to stay on good terms with the other villagers. Ahmar's father was not a particularly quarrelsome man. But the general environment in the village was such that people did not live in harmony. Nobody was ready to compromise, and people would argue over every small issue. Ahmar really hated these peasant quarrels. Soon he made his decision and stopped all contact with home so that he could study in peace. No longer would he visit his village. Ahmar said: 'I would even refuse to take money from my father. My mother would then send me money, she would motivate me, would keep praying for me.' During the two months of summer vacation, he didn't return to his village but stayed with friends in Karachi. There he prepared the topics for his course the following term by studying at a library where others studied for the CSS (Central Superior Services, the civil service in Pakistan). Ahmar helped them with English language and he learnt a lot from them. '*Docendo discimus*', as the Latin proverb says: 'By teaching we learn'. He also attended lectures and seminars organized by the Higher Education Commission of Pakistan and benefited greatly from those. Ahmar was determined to complete his degree with good grades. He preferred his career over the problems faced by his family in the village, and sees it as his long-term planning to end all the problems in one fell swoop.

Like Ahmar, Farwa prioritized her career and continued to stay at a hostel even after her family moved to the city, because she did not want her education to suffer. But it is also true that her family was in a stable financial position and didn't need her support. Besides, Farwa remained temperamental. She believes herself to be very straightforward, in the sense that she does not hide her views and calls a spade a spade, especially in her professional life. Her boss calls her 'expressive' and told her, 'You say it out when you dislike something and you say even when you like it.' Farwa talks of filters (usually of relationships) through which we see the world and the world sees us. She thinks it is the cultural filter that forces us to behave in certain ways. Our thoughts, attitudes and behaviours are filtered through customs, values and relationships. We are expected to act and react in a certain way. We are cautious about doing something because we are afraid of people's reactions. But Farwa did not care about other people's views and reactions, and she regretted nothing she had done. She, too, strongly believes in Tagore's aphorism that 'one cannot cross the sea merely by standing and staring at the water', so she always took courage and followed her heart's desire.

## *Respect and praise*

Farwa's only regret was that her early schooling had been a mess. Her mother was always concerned about her schooling and used to say that things should not be the way they were. Farwa's parents, and especially her father, worked hard to improve her behaviour and promote learning, sitting with her to help her study. Her parents gave her advice, arranged private lessons for her, tried the carrot-and-stick approach by rewarding her with toys and by punishing her. But it was all in vain: whatever her parents or teachers said fell on deaf ears. Was Farwa a lost cause like Twain's Huckleberry Finn?

Not really. The turning point came when Farwa was in class 3, aged about nine. The class monitor was absent, so her teacher asked her if *she* would like to make a speech on Independence Day and she promptly agreed. She won the first prize of story books. 'That was the start of my career,' says Farwa. 'I started feeling worthy of attention. I felt I was important. I started feeling that I could do something.' Farwa thinks that recognition, approval and self-esteem are the social needs of any person, and they are as important for survival as eating and drinking. She started comparing herself to her Adi, her elder sister, and realized that her Adi was much more liked than she, Farwa, was. People loved and cared for Adi. Adi had a reputation for being 'a good girl'. That reputation was like a label – and it predisposed people in favour of Adi. Farwa started using Adi as a role model. She also followed the example of her cousins, who used to receive praise for whatever they did when they were children. Her aspiration to be accepted and respected by people around her has made her a professor today, though she thinks that she is still not like Adi, who is a successful doctor.

The participants seemed to have struggled to gain acceptance and respect in their close circle since early in their lives. When his mother slapped him, Ahmar decided to go to school. This is a unique example of a child of 4 or 5 years old realizing that he is not being respected in his own house because he does not go to school. A great motivating factor later on was preserving self-respect; when the teacher made a rule that anyone who did not do their homework would be slapped by a class-fellow (corporal punishment is common in schools in Pakistan, however negatively it might affect children's confidence and self-esteem). An important reason to continue his education was that Ahmar knew that he would not earn any respect by being what he was. Finally, when a policeman hit him in his late teens, he decided to become a district police officer or join the armed forces. Ahmar's interview reminded me of William Blake's poem 'Infant Sorrow' (*Songs of Experience*, 1794) and the woes of living evoked by Blake and experienced by Ahmar. However, here he is, a lieutenant in the Pakistan Air Force.

A desire to be appreciated and esteemed by people around them is present in all the participants, though to varying degrees and in different ways. Farhana, for instance, experienced workplace harassment and gender-based discrimination. Whenever she arrived at a new posting, everyone in the office would come to stare at the new 'girl wonder'. On such occasions she wished she were a man and had all their freedom and that no one would stare at her. On one posting, she and another woman were sent to do field work in a site area all alone, 'just two of us with no security or anything. Just us two girls.' During another posting, one of the senior officials irritated her, coming to her office every now and then and sitting for a long time doing nothing. So, overall her experience of working life, of society outside her village, of people in general was pretty negative. Farhana expected respect outside the home as well as in it so she refused to accept the things as they were:

> I have a very strong faith in Allah. All the girls would tell me that I would lose the job. Like if officers would do something wrong, then I would say it is wrong; if it's wrong, then it is. They would tell that you would get fired but I had so much faith in Allah that this can never happen. When something is going to happen it would happen in its time. If I am to lose my job, then it can be done only by Allah. No one else can do that. I have never felt helpless. I have a strong faith in Allah.

### *Duty*

Whatever Abdur Razzak is and is not today is because he always preferred his family over all. While he was still in 6th grade, his father got him a job with a motorbike mechanic. Abdur Razzak continued his studies while working there, which was hard. After returning from school, he went to his job, working till late at night. When at last he got home at 9.00, 10.00 or even 11.00 p.m., he studied in preparation for school. Then conflict arose between his studies and his work. One day, the mechanic told Abdur Razzak to come to work in the morning as well, or leave the job so that a full-timer could be employed instead. Abdur Razzak had to choose between earning money – for immediate benefit – and going to school – for long-term benefit. He was like Hercules at the crossroads, a young man facing Pleasure personified and Virtue personified and having to choose which of the two allegorical figures should guide him through life. Hercules chose Virtue, Abdur Razzak chose education and Herculean labours lay ahead of him.

For around a year he was without a regular job. He picked up some money here and there as best he could. Sometimes he worked as a casual labourer on a construction site, and sometimes as an agricultural labourer. That's how he earned money to feed his family while still attending school in the mornings. His whole life changed. He was no longer emotional, he didn't quarrel at home over small things and he no longer had petty wishes. He became sober and determined, his mind rationally and entirely focused on his education and long-term career prospects. One day, the principal of his school saw him working as a labourer on a construction site, and offered him a job as a clerk at the school once he had passed his SSC. Abdur Razzak accepted this offer and continued his studies while working as a school clerk.

Abdur Razzak aspired to graduate from university. He gained admission but after studying there for a month or so, his father told him that he was needed at home for security reasons. His family did not force him, however, but let him decide freely whether to soldier on or to leave university. Once again Abdur Razzak was at the crossroads. He decided to leave. Meanwhile his friends from school were university students, but he was leaving. How did he feel at that moment?

> No, not exactly like everything was ending but more like something was slipping out of my hands, as you hold sand in your hands and you realise that it was slowly and gradually going out of your hands. I was thinking education was going out of my hands like that. But no, it was not utter despair, I was not totally left alone – the principal of my school, who had helped me through my Intermediate exam, continued to support me and gave me hope.

So he returned to his earlier job and is still working as a clerk in the same school. He plans to go abroad to earn more money for the sake of his family, as soon as his younger brothers take up the responsibilities at home.

When it came to supporting his family, Ahmar was careful from the beginning. As they grew older, none of his brothers showed any interest in taking care of their fields; Ahmar, however, did. In order to be a financial help to his father, he worked in the fields before sunrise. His wheat crop, especially, needed a lot of care. He then walked 5 or 6 km to school and walked home during the heat of the afternoon, when people tend to stay indoors. Before sunset he worked again in the fields and at night he studied. That was typical during summer. In 'winter', the sun sets earlier, and there is not much time to work in the fields before sunset. So Ahmar would have worked in the fields for only a short period as in villages people don't usually stay outdoors after sunset. When Ahmar grew up and had more responsibility in his household, he, unlike the other villagers, did not allow the women in his household to work in the fields. He didn't approve of that.

Ahmar's life was just one big obstacle course. He got no support from his family. He took such pains, worked so hard at school and in the fields and received no praise or appreciation. His parents didn't realize that they should spare him unnecessary worry by keeping family and village quarrels and problems away from him so that he could concentrate on his studies. So he bore the double burden of his studies and of his family and village affairs. He simply had to shed one of these burdens – either his home or his studies. He decided to give priority to his home and leave education. 'After having graduated from secondary school [SSC],' Ahmar said, 'my interest in studying died. My problems increased, the fields had to be looked after, my parents had lots of worries, so I thought of quitting my education.'

Ahmar decided to provide the support his family needed by working in the fields and dealing with village quarrels.

Farhana also faced hard times when she had to decide between self and family, although she tried to prove a help to her family. She took the responsibility of getting groceries and the maintenance of their house in the city as soon as she got a job. She always wishes that if she were a boy, she would have proved more helpful for the family and would definitely have gone abroad to earn a better living for her family.

However, Shabana's entire life has been a struggle between personal gains and those of her family. Her decision to get a divorce appeared personal and rebellious. Yet in the long run it proved to be a sacrifice on behalf of her family, as she has taken responsibility for her siblings. She thinks she will not marry, but just get her sisters married and her brothers educated. She literally runs the family and has taken the entire burden on herself. She has given her family courage.

## Family and relationships

Relations are very important in the lives of all my participants; they are both their strength and their burdens. All the participants faced times in their lives when they had to choose between their personal benefit and that of the family and made great sacrifices (see Figure 5.2).

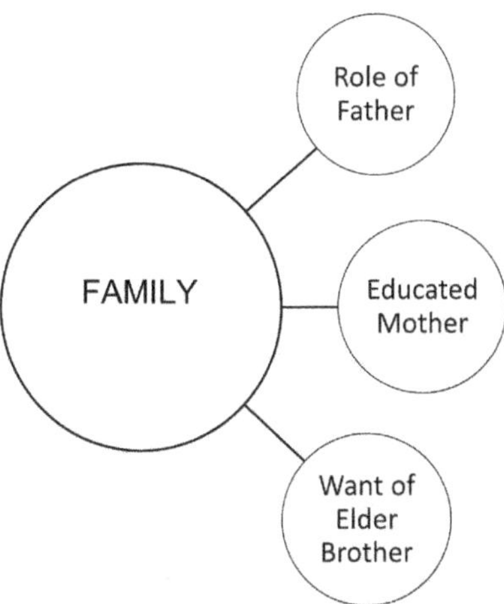


**Figure 5.2:** Family

### *The role of the father*

The father is the dominant figure in the life of each participant except for Shabana, whose mother is dominant. Shabana loves her mother more than anyone and would choose her mother above anyone else. Her mother is her inspiration for tackling so many problems in her life.

The other four participants are all attached to their fathers. Abdur Razzak talks of his father throughout his interview, starting it by saying: 'I was born in Samdhan [name of village], my father brought me up, my parents.' His father is the reason behind all his important decisions in life, and is present everywhere, from 'bringing him up', 'taking him to school', 'telling him to stay at home or go out to play', to 'asking him to quit education', 'doing a job', 'getting married' and everything else. He told me:

> My life changed due to my education and my father is responsible for getting me educated and bringing me to this stage of life. Even now I am thankful to him but if he were alive, he would have got me more education.

Ahmar said that 'I had two driving forces, one was competition and the other my father's motivation. My mother had asked me to study that first day.' Ahmar's mother slapped him for not going to school and told him that he would not be allowed to stay at home forever; he felt so bad about it that he decided never to think about skipping school, come what may, and after that 'she hadn't asked anything from me, she knew that I was doing it right on my own. My father kept a check and balance on me.' His father was very concerned about the children's well-being. And it was his father who took him to the University of Sindh to get him enrolled.

Unlike Shabana, the other women participants, Farwa and Farhana, also fondly discuss the love and support of their fathers throughout their lives. Farhana describes her father as very loving and affectionate, and said he never let them feel that he had too many daughters. She is more attached to her father than to anyone else in the family. Despite having no girls' school in the village, her father was so keen on the education of his children that they all studied in a boys' school (where he was a teacher). He got all his children educated to Masters level. When she sat in front of the parliament to protest against the government decision to expel people from their jobs and was taken to police station with the others, her father was her biggest supporter.

So it was with Farwa, who says, 'my father has always given more importance to his daughters than his sons.' Though her mother has played a significant role in her life because her father was often away from home due to his job, he always supported her and loved her more than her elder sister even, who was the 'good girl' of the family.

### *Educated mother*

An educated mother seems to be one of the most important factors in the career building of my participants. The mothers of all three female participants are educated and came from more educated families than their fathers do. The mothers who are educated and from educated families are a positive support for each of the female participants.

Farwa's mother has played a more important role in her life than her father. She was very concerned about the education of all of her children. And 'despite being girls [Farwa and her elder sister], our parents invested in our education, unlike many people even today.'

Likewise, Shabana's parents, especially her mother, were very concerned about her schooling. She and her siblings were not allowed to stay at home for a single day, even if they were ill. And their mother would not take them to any weddings or other ceremonies in the village, because they continue until late and the children's schoolwork would suffer. Shabana mentions that she started attending weddings and other late night parties in the village only after she passed her Intermediate (equivalent to A-levels). For some time after that she could not even recognize her close relatives. Despite opposition from her in-laws, her father decided that she would continue her education after Matriculation (equivalent to GCSEs).

Neither Abdur Razzak's nor Ahmar's mother is educated. And nor are their sisters as a consequence.

### *Want of an elder brother*

Except Ahmar, none of my participants has an elder brother and each greatly feels the absence of one. The want of an elder brother has caused great loss of career and social opportunities for Abdur Razzak, Farhana and Shabana.

The birth of each of the three female participants was not welcome, as the families expected and wanted a boy. This perhaps made Farwa stubborn and assertive, bold and rebellious, though she does not think it is the reason for her nature.

Farhana believes that if she had an elder brother, she would be a doctor today. Because she didn't have one, no one could go with her to the city to take the exams for the subjects that she wanted to re-sit in order to improve her scores to gain admission to the medical college. And she has felt the need of an elder brother on many occasions when the outside world is involved. She felt that an elder brother would have been her answer to the harassing eyes of male colleagues at work. Having such bitter experiences in the practical world, Farhana wished she were a boy.

Shabana suffered at every incident, and wished either to be a boy or to have an elder brother. She had an elder step-brother but he didn't own them and was more trouble than a help. Shabana thinks that her in-laws were able to cause problems and torment them only because Shabana doesn't have a young male family member on her side: an elder brother. And even today, she has to continue her struggle, get her younger sisters married and younger brothers educated, only because she has taken the responsibilities that would fall on the elder son of the family.

Of all the participants Abdur Razzak suffered most for lacking an elder brother. As his father was old when he was born, Abdur Razzak had to assume the responsibilities of the house sooner than others do. He had to start doing a job when he was very young. His father even asked him to quit education when he was in 8th class, but he carried on while also working. He could not complete his studies as he had to stay home. He wouldn't have been responsible for everything at home had he had an elder brother. He wishes his elder sisters were his brothers.

## Society

This is not just how people in the villages conceptualize gender and education, but also how men see the role of women in their households and the world around them in their village. And it is how village women see things themselves (see Figure 5.3).

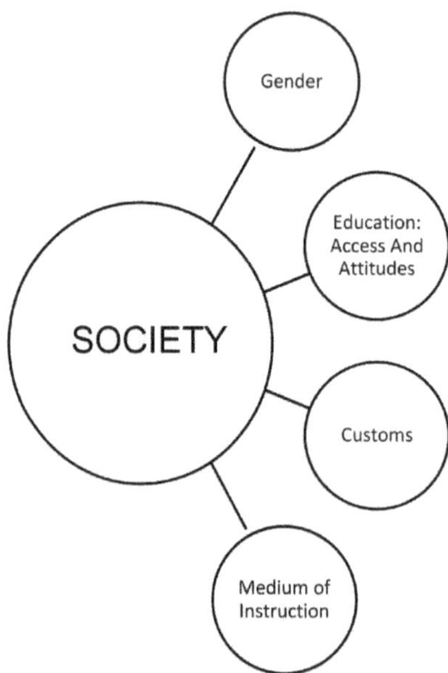


**Figure 5.3:** Society

### *The different attitudes towards girls and boys*

Parents of a boy are always proud whereas daughters are seen as a burden in the society my participants belong to. Pakistani society is generally male dominated and Sindhi culture also defines man as the head of the house and dominant in all decisions. Farwa describes it thus:

> We make a man a MAN through a lot of struggle and effort so that he knows that he is a male, he is dominant, to the extent that he may not be a human but he should be a male. Women only become important when they are mothers of sons.

Farwa is one of four children, two girls and two boys. That sounds balanced and acceptable even for a family in Pakistan. But the sequence of births also matters. The first two children were girls, Farwa the second. The first girl was a disappointment since a boy would have been preferred. But the second girl, Farwa, was a disaster, because at this stage both the children were girls. Therefore, the elderly female members of the family were not happy about Farwa's birth:

> My mother basically is an educated woman. She was fine with it. It was not like she was happy, even she was expecting a boy and she was not happy to see a baby girl. But then she thought that whatever happens is from God. So even if it is a baby girl then that's okay. So when my grandmothers would grumble as to why it was a girl, she would say the same to them as well. My mother tells me that whenever she held me in her arms saying BISMILLAH ['In the name of God, the Most Gracious, the Most Merciful', the prayer with which we should start all our actions and entrust them to Allah] or she hugged or kissed me, then my grandmothers would taunt her and say she shouldn't be so happy as she has given birth to a girl and not a boy.

It was with the birth of her first son, born five years after Farwa, that her mother started gaining 'worth' and significance in the family – as is the norm. 'My mother also became very positive; the disparaging attitudes of people because she was the mother of only girls decreased.' Farwa's mother loved Farwa as a mother should, but was somehow unconsciously inattentive towards her.

The data shows that gender-based expectations vary from village to village. In the case of both Farwa and Farhana, the environment in their villages was not very strict towards little girls. Farwa was allowed as a child to play with boys and her best friends have always been from both genders. Both Farwa and Farhana used to play out of the house until late in the evening, swimming and bathing in the brook, cycling, climbing trees and so on. Both also identify that their attitudes are more like those of boys. This generates the idea that certain attitudes and behaviours are attributed to each gender. Besides, both of them were scolded and beaten for their naughtiness and Farwa especially was not accepted because of her rebellious behaviour. While discussing this, Farwa says:

> Every culture has its own customs, its own norms. In our culture with relevance to gender the norms are that there is no space for rebellious attitude of girls, for not listening to what is being said there is no acceptance.

Attitudes towards girls are deeply conservative in Shabana's village: girls are supposed to get married and suffer at the hands of their in-laws. They do not have a say in anything. Besides, should they be taught in university 'they would definitely elope with somebody someday' because it is perceived that it will give them freedom that would be too much for them. Shabana's attitude and eagerness for education was laughed at. And people were sure that she would give the family a bad name.

The role of women in their household is very clearly defined by both my male participants as if they were cardboard characters in a play or novel with no real life, let alone multidimensional personalities. They are there to do household chores, prepare meals and take care of all the needs of children and the males of the household. Ahmar mentions that women from other houses in their village work in fields, though he does not like this and does not ask the women in the house to do so.

On the question about the education of girls, Abdur Razzak remarked that basic reading and writing are enough for women. Ahmar, however, simply laughed and said that the circumstances are so bad for male education in his village that the question of female education does not arise. Therefore, as in things, in the case of education, men are prioritized.

Although, like all the participants, Farhana wished to be esteemed, she also experienced workplace harassment and gender-based discrimination. After an unsatisfactory posting, she was soon transferred to another office, but that was no better. The new boss was rude to her. Colleagues with friends in high places were promoted to become managers or coordinators and then started being arrogant and needlessly insulted Farhana and the colleagues who had no political backing. All the girls except Farhana and her village friend were given office work. She was not only the victim of male prejudice, but also the victim of the disdain in which condescending, haughty city girls hold village girls, however well-qualified they might be. So the city women working at this office would take sides with the boss against the village women, tell gossips and disparage them to harm their reputations. Overall, her experience of working life, of society outside her village and of people in general, was pretty negative. Her experience of work reminded me of Brecht's cutting verses from the *Threepenny Opera* (1931):

> What nourishes man?
> Every hour
> He tortures another human being, robs him of his clothes,
> attacks him, strangles him, yea devours him.
> The only way man lives is by being able
> To forget so thoroughly that he too is a human being.
> Listen, gentlemen, don't indulge in wishful thinking,
> Man survives only by committing crimes.

### *Access to and attitudes towards education*

People in Pakistan often accuse village teachers of being lazy, of not trying to teach well, nor caring whether their pupils actually learn anything but only wanting to collect their salaries. These critics see this as the reason why village children know and can do less than town and city children and why they fail when they have to compete with them in later education. Farhana does not agree with that reasoning. Though teaching methods in the village and in the city are quite different, especially in the teaching of English, Farhana feels that village teachers should not bear all the blame for the inferior performance of their pupils. It is also, she claims, the fault of the children and their families. She maintains: 'A child who truly wants to learn can learn even in the worst village school; but a child who does not want to learn will fail even in the best city school and with the best teachers.' To support Farhana's view, I would tell them the famous story of Ekalavya from the *Mahabharata*, the ancient Indian epic.

Despite having access to education, people in the villages are not very positive about the education of their children. Both private and government schooling is available to people in Abdur Razzak's village, but the significance of education was so poorly understood that his own father asked him several times to quit school. Similarly, separate schools for boys and girls exist in Shabana's village yet hardly any people are educated. Shabana studied in a private co-educational school – which was free because her father was a teacher of Qur'an there; other people would not send their daughters to even a free government school only because a boys' school was very nearby. Moreover, people from her village were so conservative that when she went to university for her studies, they said she 'would elope with somebody soon'.

Though the environment of Farhana's village was not otherwise conservative towards girls, it was not open to female education, mainly because the girls were not interested. But that could be because they were not encouraged. The village had no girls' school so Farhana studied in a boys' school.

Ahmar's village also had just one primary school, which people used to tie their cattle up to and store their fodder. A discouraging attitude prevailed towards those who wanted to study. Most villagers thought that once the younger generation were educated, they would be out of control and no longer listen to their elders. It reminds me of Shakespeare's *Henry VI, Part 2* (1594), where the Clerk of Chatham is hanged as a traitor because he can write his name. It was no doubt realized that education can secure a better living, yet instead of giving their own children this opportunity, people were more interested in stopping, misguiding and creating trouble for those receiving education. Ahmar's uncles stopped giving them money, quarrelled with them and created many problems in order to prevent their studying.

### *Village customs*

Village customs have left deep marks on the lives of my participants. Shabana especially suffered because the elders put her into *nikah* (a marriage contract) when she was just five days old; and also tried to stop her in the name of honour when she decided to break her wedlock and free herself of all chains. Unlike Shabana, her mother had accepted sacrificing her life for the honour of her family and married a man thrice her age when she was still very young.

Abdur Razzak's father's second marriage at an advanced age because he had no children from his first wife is not unusual. Likewise, in his brother's marriage, the girl's parents ask for a bride price from him in exchange for their daughter – the opposite to the custom of dowry, which is also common and regarded as essential even in cities. Jamal Abro, a fine writer of modern fiction in Sindhi, castigates the custom of bride price as a social evil in his novel *Pirani* (1959).

Childhood marriages and marriages of very young girls to older men, which effectively prevent children from leaving home for education or employment and show little respect to people who are physically or financially weak, are not specific to certain villages but are part of everyday Sindhi life. Where, on the one hand, Sindhis are known for their hospitality to friends and foes alike, on the other hand, we see jealousy at anyone's success, leg-pulling and back-biting as common characteristics.

### *Medium of instruction at schools*

Issues of language are complex in this province, especially in relation to basic education in the villages. All primary education in rural areas is in Sindhi. Urdu and English are introduced at later stages. But in cities, it differs from city to city and sometimes school to school. And in some private schools, Sindhi language or literature is not taught at all and Sindhi is not the medium of instruction.

Though all the participants faced problems related to language, Ahmar discusses them specifically. He notes that in the villages especially, but generally in government schools in Sindh (although not in other provinces), primary education is in Sindhi, and English letters are introduced from 6th grade. However, students coming to the university from education in the cities, notes Farhana, are ahead in English language and therefore the students from villages lose out. In addition to Sindhi and English, the secondary language of Urdu complicates the issue still further.

## Note

[1] King Richard II of England was 15 when, in 1382, he married his first wife, Anne of Bohemia, aged 16. After she died, he married again, in 1396. His new wife was Isabella of Valois, aged 6. He was 28 by then. Also, St Elizabeth of Hungary (Elizabeth of Thuringia) (1207–31) was promised in marriage when she was 4 years old.

*Chapter 6*

# Striving for improvement: Hearing the voices of mature students

*Teresa Bruen*

> *Our struggle is to discover new methods, to help us find our way through the tangle of human thought to the 'drivers' that govern our actions. (Hart, 1996: 63)*

Educational research and the methodologies employed therein have changed significantly over time. The qualitative turn in educational research developed from a search for meaning that could not be explored through quantitative methods alone. Narrative research is becoming increasingly popular within the field of educational practice and experience (Clandinin and Connelly, 2000). It is used to recreate and communicate experiences, feelings and places. My decision to employ a narrative approach reflects the importance of placing the person and their narrative at the heart of the enquiry, signifying the importance of their stories. The concept of experience is key, and narrative allows for the capturing of experience in a way that is unrestricted for the mature students, allowing them to tell their story without the limitations of closed questions or questionnaires. Polkinghorne (1988) asserted that people without narratives do not exist, and I believe that stories are at the heart of our lives. Connolly and Clandinin (1990) suggest:

> Humans are story telling organisms who, individually and collectively, lead storied lives. Thus, the study of narrative is the study of the ways humans experience the world.

My enquiry is situated in a real-world setting and aims to build an in-depth understanding of the experiences of mature students in relation to the field of higher education. The use of a narrative approach allows them the space to recount their personal stories in relation to their educational experiences using their own words to emphasize what is significant for them. The telling of a story links events through the unilinear passage of time from past to present to the future and identifies the effects of choices, linking a prior choice or happening to a later effect. Clandinin and Connolly (2000) recommend using the terms 'personal' and 'social'. These explore the interaction between past, present and future to demonstrate continuity and combine these with the notion of space which in essence contains the situation.

The concept of multivoicedness is also important throughout this narrative enquiry. Scholars recognize that there are voices and not just one lone voice. Therefore I was cognizant that although I recognize that narratives are personal stories and individual and unique to each student, they are also in essence collective stories formed by the cultural, historical and institutional settings in which they take place (Elbaz-Luwisch, 1997). Recounting experiences in narrative form does not take place in isolation; I was aware throughout the relating of the stories of the social context in which these students found themselves; their backgrounds, lives and families, and their commitments outside the field of education. This has a certain fit with Bourdieu's concepts of capital, habitus and field.

Freeman (1984) suggested that in the case of narrative story, causal linkage of events is sometimes only discovered retrospectively. Certain events that may have seemed insignificant at the time may have actually been crucial in affecting overall outcomes (Polkinghorne, 1995). This became clear as the students recounted their stories and then seemed to have a moment of enlightenment when they managed to connect events in the past to present-day situations or feelings.

It was of the utmost importance to me that my participants would be interested and willing to share their stories, and in this I was extremely fortunate. I met them within year two of the programme and explained the concept of the research and how they would be telling their own story in relation to their experiences of higher education. I left it sitting with them to discuss and think about, giving them supporting documentation that confirmed what the research was about, what it entailed and the way ethical issues such as anonymity and confidentiality would be handled.

Following that explanation, six students approached me to say they were interested in being part of the research and sharing their stories. As it happens, there was an even gender divide, as three men and three women came forward. They were excited and enthusiastic and passionately wanted to share their story and be part of a study that demonstrated their individuality and its significance within the field of education.

Because the students came forward voluntarily to share their stories, this research, in effect, is theirs: it is the tale of their collective journeys to overcome restrictive educational access and inequality, thereby ensuring through higher education a better lifestyle for themselves and their families. I am forever grateful to the six participants who, no matter how time-pressured they were – and they most certainly were, constantly – gave of their time in a generous and above all truthful fashion.

Significantly, narrative research is a fluid enquiry and it was consequently essential that I engage in ongoing reflection throughout the process. I found this quite difficult at times. I had to engage in a deeply meaningful manner with my own preconceptions and presumptions, made initially at the very genesis of this research enquiry and well before actually commencing it.

One of my presumptions was that being a mature student myself meant I was the same as the participants. I quickly discarded this notion once I listened to and reflected on their narratives. Of course there were some similarities, but their backgrounds and stories were very different to my own. Keeping a considered and authentic reflective journal enabled me to address my preconceptions and be mindful and considerate of the narratives presented to me.

Narrative is used to recreate experiences, feelings and places. While the concept of experience was key to this investigation, it was essential that experience was captured in a way that didn't restrict the participants and allowed their stories to be told in full without the limits that closed questions and restrictive questionnaires impose. I believe that narrative enquiry allows true communication as the person and their story are always central.

The rationale for using a narrative methodology for this enquiry was that the students were at the centre of my enquiry; it was their voices, so long silenced, that I wished to bring to the fore.

So here is a brief pen portrait of each of the participants. It is followed by discussion of the various themes that emerge from their narratives and direct quotes from their stories, which shine through and lift off the page, giving us profound insight into their meanings and experiences, and their lives. It is their shared voices you hear, not mine, and they are always central to the research. As Seamus Heaney famously observed: 'If you have the words, there's always a chance that you'll find the way.'

Throughout my chapters in this book the reader will appreciate the complexities and characters of the participant, but first I introduce them briefly. Their names have been changed to protect their identity.

## Delia

Delia is a 48-year-old woman who has followed a diverse and interesting career pathway. She was born in England to Irish parents, the third of four children: three girls and a boy. Her family returned to Ireland when she was 14, and she was enrolled in a vocational school in a rural location in the

West of Ireland. After completing school to Leaving Certificate standard she was accepted by a regional technical college to study art.

For financial reasons, however, Delia did not complete her studies and migrated to London where she was employed in various jobs, such as waitressing. Some years later she returned to her home town and married a farmer. They have three children: two girls and a boy. Her two younger children are in secondary school and the oldest daughter is studying applied social sciences in college. Delia worked with marginalized, vulnerable groups such as asylum seekers, employing her skills as an African drummer and artist to engage with people. It was this involvement with vulnerable groups and her strong sense of social justice that gave her the impetus to return to education. She felt that a degree in applied social studies would equip her with the knowledge and skills needed to help vulnerable individuals, families and communities.

## Noreen

Noreen is a 47-year-old married woman. She has five children and is foster mother to another three. She provides emergency placement for children within the Health Services Executive. Noreen completed her Leaving Certificate but performed poorly. She moved to London with her boyfriend, became pregnant with her first child and married at 19. In London she worked part-time as a waitress. She returned to Ireland and became involved in the provision of childcare. She engaged with educational programmes at certificate level in relation to childcare and progressed to enrol in an undergraduate programme in applied social studies.

## Joseph

Joseph is 33 years old. He is in a relationship with a fellow student and they are expecting their first child together. Joseph left school before completing his Leaving Certificate and worked in unskilled jobs in Ireland and abroad. In telling his story Joseph revealed that he had been addicted to alcohol but has been sober now for some years. Because he was interested in working with vulnerable and marginalized people, he decided to undertake the degree programme in applied social studies.

## Geraldine

Geraldine is 33 years old. She is separated from her husband and has a three-year-old son. She is in a new relationship and expecting a child. Geraldine was in foster care for most of her childhood and at one time was homeless. She did not complete her second-level education and, as a result, has no formal educational qualifications. Her childhood was difficult and because of frequently moving from foster home to residential care, she couldn't settle in school.

## Kenneth

Kenneth is a 45-year-old single man. He lives with his elderly father who has a disability and is his father's primary carer. Kenneth is one of 14 children and helped his father work on their farm from a young age. Kenneth attended school until he was 14 and then left to work full-time on the farm. The emphasis in the household was on hard labour and little attention was paid to schoolwork. He also worked in casual employment in unskilled jobs. His reason for entering education is that he felt he had missed out and that he could achieve more academically, given the right opportunity.

## Ivan

Ivan is a 36-year-old man who lives with his partner, Terence. One of six children, he lived on a farm in rural Ireland. He worked on the farm, sometimes to the detriment of his schoolwork. He found school difficult partly because he had dyslexia, which was not diagnosed until he was 34. Ivan recounted that he was encouraged by his teachers to leave school and start work, so left school at 15 with no formal qualifications and was engaged in unskilled work for some years in Ireland and abroad. He returned to Ireland keen to enter higher education to gain a qualification and develop a challenging and rewarding career.

So this is the brief outline of the lives and backgrounds of my research participants. However, they are so much more than these introductory paragraphs can describe. All have fascinating life histories that they graciously shared with me during the interviews.

## Not-so-common histories

This chapter draws together the commonalities and themes that resonated through the narratives of the participants. The themes were constructed manually through careful reading and re-reading, while carefully identifying commonalities across the six narratives. At times the stories were remarkably similar but what was particularly apparent in all their stories was the theme of struggle and the great sense of injustice. Yet these stories are not without a happy ending – wait and see. While listening to their narratives I was reminded of James Joyce's words: 'Your battles inspired me – not the obvious material battles but those that were fought and won behind your forehead.'

The centrality of their voices is crucial so I want them to resonate strongly and clearly throughout this chapter and I aim to accomplish that by quoting their own words.

## Self

What was it about these students that made them come forward to be part of this research? The literature suggests the decision of mature students to enter the field of higher education is multifaceted and 'fragile' (Davies and Williams, 2001) and that they give it a great deal of consideration first. Osborne et al. (2004: 295) propose that it entails 'a complete reorientation of lifestyle'. This is because the mature student has to fulfil other commitments, such as caring and domestic duties, while engaging with higher education. The literature shows that reasons for returning to education are varied and may be interrelated; they can change at any time depending on the individual student's circumstances (Cree et al., 2009; Reay et al., 2002; Osborne et al., 2004; Kettley, 2007). Contemporary literature also suggests that embarking on study at a mature age is of value to the individual student, their family and to wider society.

Among the many issues they spoke about, the sense of struggle was central. The students had struggled throughout their lives, especially in relation to their education. This thread, this concept of struggle was omnipresent. I suggest that the concept of struggle was the backdrop to all the stories told.

Throughout the narratives there was a firm sense of identifying their experiences with their earliest memories of their time spent in primary and secondary school. The impact of their experiences strongly assaulted the very essence of their self. It left a resounding impression upon each of them, to the extent that they had lost belief in themselves and begun to think they could not function at school. Certain sub-themes were common to their experiences.

## Negative experiences of primary and secondary school

All six of these narratives dwelt on the informants' negative experiences of school. It was an overwhelmingly powerful indicator of their experiences, thoughts and feelings in relation to their education. As each person told their story it became apparent in the tone of their voices, the sincerity of their words, the expressions on their faces and their body language that recounting these memories made them sad, frustrated and at times angry. These past experiences offended their very sense of self. They all expressed strong feelings of injustice that impacted upon their sense of being and left a resounding and lasting mark upon them – they felt inadequate, not good enough, stupid.

Geraldine spoke about how she was made to feel by the teachers, 'Well, oh I knew I was stupid, that's the way I looked at it.'

Delia described similar experiences: 'What I was really good at was never ever nurtured, so in my years of secondary school I would have felt that I was not smart, that I was not intelligent.' Delia believed that she and others were treated unjustly within the educational system: 'I remember at the time feeling a sense of injustice and I really do, and I remember clearly you know feeling that sense of injustice back in the convent.' She went on: 'coming to Ireland ... let me think, the difference in the educational system here in Ireland ... I didn't get educated here at all actually.'

Kenneth talked about his experience of secondary school: 'You know when I went to secondary school I'd say I fell a little behind at that stage.' However, this issue was not addressed by the teachers even though Kenneth recounted that he didn't work at school and rarely completed his homework. He recalled, 'I don't think I ever did any homework in the school.'

Noreen remembered that, 'Having been in school previously it had not been a pleasurable experience, shall we say, or a successful experience.'

It is interesting that when asked about their experiences of education, all the participants immediately spoke about negative ones, beginning very early in primary school and following these through to their time spent in secondary school. Wright (2011) suggests that the negative experiences of schooling have a lasting effect and this was especially true for these mature students. They remembered the negative experiences in detail and became visibly upset while recounting them.

These experiences were still extremely significant to them; they were still very raw and upset about that time in their lives. They also felt incredulous that they could have been treated with such disrespect, such lack of care, because of their socio-economic status. They were country children from poor rural backgrounds with parents who had had little or no education. Wright (2011) identified the importance of earlier educational experience for mature women in terms of their ability to achieve, how they were or were not motivated to engage with further study, and how this affected their confidence about returning to education as an adult. Those students who had unpleasant experiences of the compulsory sector were especially nervous. Their expectations of higher education were that they would be treated similarly. Reay (2002: 407) would refer to this as 'troubled educational history'.

As they recounted their narratives, I was reminded that they were only small children at that time, burdened with spending a significant part of their young lives in a space that made them very unhappy, through no fault of their own.

## Relationships with teachers

Young children's relationships with teachers in early education can have a significant effect on their life chance. A positive role model in the form of a much loved and admired teacher has a lasting impact upon a child and can often make the difference as to whether or not they will succeed academically and, if they do, add immensely to the students' self-worth.

Four of the students described how their relationships with their teachers added to the overall negative experiences of their early education. Ivan talked about how he felt he was bullied by the principal of the primary school:

> Myself and the principal would have had a major clash over sport, where he was big into hurling and I had absolutely no interest. And I honestly think that ended up clouding my whole experience of education even because for me anyway I would have put him down as a bully, just different things that he said like 'a small lad like you'. I ended up having height issues for a long time after and it was stupid things like that that turned me off.

He recounted how the principal behaved towards him when he handed up his homework. He recalled:

> Like that principal always had issues about how badly you did it like and he would kinda make sure that everyone in the class knew definitely like and I was talking to a friend of mine recently and she said that he definitely had a thing against me and that it wasn't in my head like.

The students' habitus did not fit comfortably within the field of education and this suggests that they were uncomfortable, and felt that they didn't belong. Mills and Gale (2007: 436) suggest that Bourdieu used the term habitus to mean:

> recurring patterns of class outlook – the beliefs, values conduct, speech, dress and manners – which are inculcated by habitus in terms of everyday experiences within the family, the peer group and the school.

The working-class background of the students was not recognized or appreciated by the teachers in the schools they attended and this added to the students' sense of unhappiness and not fitting in.

Geraldine stated that her teachers had told her: 'You will amount to nothing, you're one of those kids that hangs around street corners and that's what you will be for your life' – and that stuck with her.

She said that the teachers had no belief in her ability or potential to achieve academically:

> They only seen my past and where I was, social workers, residential care and all that adds up to being trouble. When I received my junior cert' results they called everyone in to the library where you get your results and the principal actually had to go down and get the hard copy and check to see if the results were right because I had passed.

Ivan felt that he was encouraged to leave school by one of his teachers. He said:

> I was doing fourth year and a job came up which was more or less a summer job but it started a month early and my mother decided I should talk to the Careers Guidance teacher, who told me ahh yeh go for it and whatever. It was with horses and had nothing to do with education or anything, and she said why wouldn't you and a month off school sure it wouldn't do you any harm, ahh and sure you never know it might develop into a job and you might be as well of not to come back. And that was it. I just went. That really stuck in my head and I thought well he doesn't want me to come back.

A very clear message delivered and received: that school was not the right place for him, that he didn't fit in. Joseph felt that because he lived on a council estate the teachers did not expect much from him academically:

> Because you were from a council estate by association you were going to be in trouble. And it meant that you were not going to succeed in school. I felt that from the teachers.

Wright (2011) highlighted a rigid adherence to procedures and a lack of imagination demonstrated by teachers who failed to explore the reasons as to why students behaved in a certain way. Habitus enables us to understand such matters, as it persuades us to consider in relational terms rather than in opposites.

Therefore the relationship between the teachers and the structures of the organization and the effects these had on these students when they were children proved significant. Their habitus was structured through their past and present experiences and this shaped their practices and behaviours. Habitus works relationally with one's present circumstances. The teachers within the compulsory educational sector were unaware of the personal habitus of their young pupils. This lack of understanding led to certain behaviours by the children that reproduced social inequality within the educational system and created or reinforced poor relationships with teachers. This in turn impacted negatively on their experiences. Grenfell (2004) reasons that the presence of poor relationships with teachers is due to students being put in their place by things that happen in the classroom. This, he suggests, is due to a lack of connection by the students with the educational system and a disconnection with their personal habitus. It may happen by stealth in many thousands of tiny interactions, until the student is excluded or excludes themself because they have no choice.

My participants recounted many interactions where teachers implied that they didn't fit within the educational system and suggested that they wouldn't succeed at it. Some of them had had undiagnosed learning difficulties and the teachers mistook these for laziness. Their obliviousness to their pupils' cognitive habitus made for difficult relationships and negative experiences for students during their compulsory education.

## Struggle

Throughout their narratives there was a consistent theme of ongoing struggle all their lives regarding education. The word 'struggle', when used as a verb, means 'to battle', 'to compete', 'to fight' according to the *Oxford English Dictionary*. The students openly expressed their experiences of struggle, but what really emerged was their sense of accomplishment, of getting through the tough times, of managing to survive.

All the students had struggled financially and with academic challenges, such as undiagnosed learning difficulties. While some had been assessed and were eligible for learning support (known as remedial classes) they were unhappy with the idea and did not want to avail themselves of such classes.

Geraldine explains that she didn't like the stigma attached to attending remedial classes and this added to her struggle. She recalled:

> I pretended that I didn't struggle so that I wouldn't be sent again. And an awful lot I would remember the pictures. I'd read the

> story at home and I would be able to spout it back because I'd look at the pictures and I would have a fair idea.

Geraldine remained reluctant to avail herself of learning support within higher education even though she was entitled to them. The lasting effect of the stigma of the early remedial classes never left her. She worked with other students who had learning difficulties and she found solidarity and comfort within that space.

Joseph also acknowledged the stigma attached to attending remedial classes:

> There was definitely a stigma attached, yeh a stigma and my mates they didn't slag me about it but they couldn't understand how someone so smart had to go into the … and I am not being nasty about it, into the thick people's class.

Joseph talked about the behaviour of the children who attended these classes and the consequences of misbehaving within the class. The class was not meeting his needs and the stigma attached to attending these classes accumulated as reasons for him to leave the remedial class.

> And the trouble with being in there was that there was a lot of trouble within in that class. There was people in there getting in more trouble because they didn't like school, they never had a good experience of school, I don't know which but ... if you got into trouble in school then you couldn't play sport, so the quicker I got out of that the better.

All the students who attended remedial classes found them unhelpful. There seemed to be no individual learning plan for each student, so their specific learning needs were not met. This combined with the stigma attached to attending the classes and how this precipitated the bullying of one of them. In the event, the classes were unpleasant and ultimately a waste of resources. At the time of this enquiry Ivan and Joseph were availing themselves of learning support, but Geraldine refused, feeling that this was connected to her earlier negative experiences of such support.

The struggle of having undiagnosed learning difficulties was also discussed. Ivan recalled:

> But I suppose I always struggled going through school and as it turned out years later I found out that I was dyslexic but not until I got to, what, 34.

Ivan recalled the effects of academic streaming when he entered secondary level:

> Well I knew that it was gonna be a struggle you know. We would have had three grades in school, you would have had 1:1 and 1:2 and 1:3 and I would have been in the third one. You just kinda go with the attitude that I am thick you know and we are all thick together kinda unified, kinda thing like.

Ivan believes that streaming academically does not work – that it 'definitely holds the bottom rung to the bottom rung'. He suggests that the children within the lower academic classes are not challenged or exposed to those who are academically brighter and he wonders about the effect of that on him and others like him.

Kenneth had similar experiences, and recalled the class he found himself in on entering secondary school and the effect it had on him.

> Well, we were sorta in the class of dunces, and you'd sorta – well we would have picked up on that, on that energy like in the place – so I didn't apply myself at all. I don't think I ever did any homework for the school.

Financial struggles were a significant part of the students' lives. Noreen described the financial struggles that her parents had in relation to her education, especially because her father was an alcoholic. She recalled:

> and again my mother was kept on a shoestring because again it was like the little woman at home. And I suppose she had to ask for every single penny, but I suppose the bit I did resent was there was always money there for drink because even for books for money I struggled, you know I had to beg, borrow, you know and second hand which you know wasn't a problem you know, but at the start of the year I would be accommodated in that but as the year went on you know, forget it you got your books in September what are you looking for now?

Delia talks about her financial struggles while in higher education: 'A lot of people who are in the class are struggling to pay you know. There was a couple of years that we struggled, and there are a couple of people that are still struggling financially.' The struggles spoken about were multifaceted. Some of the participants were working on the family farm and this element of struggle relates to their families' overall view of education. The theme of struggle is an issue when they speak about the difficulties of balancing work, family and study commitments.

## Family and relationships

> *Ar scath a cheile a mhaireann na daine*
> (Under the shelter of each other, people survive)

This is an interesting theme as the concept of family and relationships is divided into present and past. In their early days as primary school children from a poor rural farming community, they had no support at home from their families. The dearth of 'family support' during their compulsory education was a main theme explored by all the participants. The poor cultural capital within their family networks was especially significant in determining their experiences. For all, education was not prioritized; they were from a 'farming community' so the work on the farm was the priority. Their families had not engaged with the field of education beyond what was mandatory at that time and therefore cultural capital was lacking in their homes.

The connection between parental education and children's progression to higher education is longstanding. The mature students in my study were all the first in their families to enter higher education. The literature suggests that people from a working-class background still rarely progress to higher education (Brooks, 2003). When speaking about family support in relation to their early educational experiences, these students were talking about their parents, siblings and, for one of them, her foster parents and staff at a residential home for children. The participants' narratives indicated that their inadequate family support was a deeply personal and individual experience which they had felt was unique and influenced their early experiences of education overall.

The conceptual tool of capital allows analysis of the significance of support for these students. Their families lacked the cultural capital in education to be supportive of their children during their compulsory education years and this was strongly identified in their narratives. Mills and Gale (2007) suggest that for many poor students time spent in school was irrelevant and an extravagance. Wright (2011) reported that there is a working-class expectation that after reaching the minimum school leaving age, their children should become economically independent; to have more than the basic education provided was seen as a luxury. The participants stated that their families did not expect them – and actually did not want them – to continue their education after the minimum basic requirement, illustrating the lack of cultural capital within their family environment.

Wright (2011) identifies embodied family values whereby a lower-class disinclination to invest in their children's future contrasts starkly with a middle-class value of that education as vital to a successful future. Linked to this and identified by all six students is the concept of an economic cap where school is viewed as an expensive luxury. Reay (2002) suggests that there is always an element of social class involved in educational choices and that social class is related to economic capital. These students identified themselves as being from working-class backgrounds and inherent in all their narratives was lack of economic capital.

Devine (2004) proposes that middle-class parents marshal an array of resources in a concerted effort to secure educational and ensuing occupational success for their children. For this to happen there has to be a strong family culture of valuing education. Parents have to know how to enable their children to succeed within the field of education and what resources they need to employ that will benefit their children. To achieve this they have to have certain knowledge and adequate financial resources. More importantly, they need to recognize the value of education for their children and this means having the requisite cultural, economic and social capital. Within my cohort this was not the case.

Geraldine talked about the concept of support. She was in residential care from the age of seven where she was given no support with her education, and at fifteen she was living on the streets. She spoke about what her life had been like:

> My parents are both, they both left school when they were very young so there was no support. I had no support there, homework, reading, spelling wise. With me it was kinda different because I only had parents for like the first seven years and then I went into care and when I was in care it wasn't something that was a priority in the care home, no they wouldn't go to parent teacher meetings so I didn't have anyone coming to support me from the care homes…
>
> It was up to the older children in the care home to make sure that the younger children had done their homework. So a lot of the time they just done it for us. Where they wouldn't just sit down and teach us they did it. And they done their own and they struggled in their own way because they didn't have the support either – children rearing children.

Geraldine was given a bed in a hostel on a temporary basis. She was considering returning to education but no support was provided and education was not prioritized for her within that environment. She explained:

> I wanted to go back and do something so I asked to go back. But the hostel that I was in at that time, you were only allowed to stay there for six months so just as I started back they moved me in to the Salvation Army home in Dublin. When you went in there it was like semi-independent living. You had twenty-five pounds a week and it wouldn't pay for my train pass and to go to school. So I had to leave school as it came down to a choice between food and school.

Noreen talked about her mother's inability to help with schoolwork:

> Again my mother wasn't very good at school either, and you know looking back now I would probably say that my mother had dyslexia and it wasn't picked up on then. She wasn't able to help with schoolwork at all. If anything if it came to letter writing we were writing her letters for her. And again she came from a background that as soon as you were old enough you got a job. So that was the sort of expectation in my house growing up …
>
> I suppose my father had always told me 'I was working at thirteen and sending money home to my parents.' So that was the expectation.

Kenneth told a similar story:

> Well then at home there would be no emphasis on education, at home, you know and that's being honest about it, they'd be absolutely no emphasis at all like. When I left school my father didn't bat an eyelid.

During her narrative, Noreen paused, questioning:

> I have often thought, now that I am back in education, what if I had more support what would have happened? It might have been different.

Like most of the students, Kenneth was from a farming background, and he was one of 14 children. He said:

> It was more important at home in my case, 'twas more important to milk cows and go to the bog, yeh, yeh you know because you

> know there was fourteen in the family, do you know what I mean my father and mother had come from a different generation you know?

The mature students who were from a farming background spoke about how they had an enormous amount of physical work to do on the farm before and after their days in school and this was prioritized above their schoolwork.

Reay et al. (2002) connect higher education with parents' desires for their children, and Osborne et al. (2004) found that mature students believed they would be positive role models for their children and in some cases their grandchildren.

When my participants talked about their present support from their families they were overwhelmingly positive. The picture had changed completely. All were tremendously grateful for receiving such great support from their families.

Joseph talked about the support that he received from his partner:

> She will batter me if I don't put my studies first [laughs]. Oh yeh I would be very lazy and also my sister is great she wud say 'You got more the last time, how come you didn't get the marks this time?'

Noreen talks about the support her husband gives her:

> He has taken up an awful lot of the slack. I often used to wonder what would have happened if he had been working full-time. I probably would have struggled a lot more. So he has been hugely supportive.

Delia found the support of her husband of benefit too:

> On the practical level, brilliant husband that has to be said, kids are older and all in school. There are a couple of people who support me and I have a supportive family.

Geraldine related how her partner, who is also attending college, helps her with notes:

> He gives me his notes, he has dyslexia and he is always telling me I need to be tested.

The importance of friends was identified as significant. Geraldine said:

> I think I have been lucky enough to find a click in a group and it helps an awful lot, because you support each other and not just through studies but personally as well. I find there's an awful lot of that in our course.

She talked about how learning goes on outside the college setting and how she found that to be useful:

> It continues even in the evening. Our home is like a hub, loads of us live on the same road, they would be down, they come to my house because I have kids and I can't move. The discussions often go on into the wee hours of the morning about we could do this or do that and how you tie different things in. That's what is helping a lot of us that's struggling with the reading, writing the academic side of things. We all kinda club our ideas and we get through that way.

Joseph also stressed the importance of friends, observing that:

> Since coming in here my first impression has grown like you get very good friendships like and you develop them and you get very good supports like from the friendships as well. Not a hope in hell would you get through without the friendships and supports.

Noreen also valued her friends for being supportive:

> We have a core group and we have friends. Yes I would call them friends and we go to each other's houses and we do coffee and we do stuff like that which I never thought would happen. But it has and it is lovely now because they believe, because each person knows what people can achieve do you know? And it's like they would encourage you.

Their current family and friends and supportive networks was a strong thread running through the students' narratives. This was in direct contrast to the lack of support in their earlier education, both from the institutions themselves and their immediate families at home.

## Society

> *The unfairness of allowing only certain people to succeed, based not upon merit but upon the cultural experiences, social ties and economic resources they can access, often remains unacknowledged in the broader society. (Wacquant, 1998: 216)*

It is this observation that stays with me and is the essence of this enquiry. Unfairness, injustice in the field of education was the theme that threaded through the narratives of the mature students. How do we begin to understand this so we can address it? Examining their education through the concept of Bourdieu's capital gives us a vehicle to expose the injustice of their situation. Bourdieu argues that it is the culture of the dominant group that ensures their success within the education system, so that educational differences are mistaken for academic giftedness rather than class-based differences (Bourdieu and Passeron, 1979).

The concept of cultural capital identifies the knowledge of bourgeois culture, which is unequally available within society and thus aids the preservation of social hierarchy under the guise of individual capacity and scholastic meritocracy (Wacquant, 1998). Therefore the inherent demands of the educational system, according to Bourdieu (1998: 20), 'maintain the pre-existing order, that is, the gap between pupils endowed with unequal amounts of cultural capital'.

Education is a symbolic capital and can be employed to advantage or disadvantage social actors within the field (Grenfell, 2008). The concept of capital is only valuable in terms of a 'socio-culturally defined arbitrary' construct (Grenfell, 2004: 28).

Consequently, capital needs to be understood as symbolic and not as having ultimate worth. Bourdieu suggests that symbolic capital has three principal forms: economic, social and cultural capital. This broadens the notion of capital beyond the commonly assumed economic factor towards a wider system of exchanges where diverse assets are traded within various fields (Moore, 2008). Grenfell et al. (2004) propose that all capital, be it economic, social or cultural, is symbolic and shapes social practice. They suggest that all forms of capital are derived from economic power and subsequently lead to economic outcomes. Economic capital is often articulated through social and cultural capital and therefore the economic implications often go unnoticed in social and cultural phenomena. My enquiry explores the experiences of the mature students within this context in relation to the three principal forms of symbolic capital that link them to the field of higher education and habitus.

It is capital that social agents employ to better their position within the field. Bourdieu argues that there are two ways in which symbolic capital should be understood. The first suggests that values and lifestyles of certain social groups are considered superior to those of others and as such bestow social advantage. The second effect of capital is the way forms of consciousness vary qualitatively within different social groups. Capital is an essential determinant of results for the players who enter the field to play the game. It can enhance their opportunities and maximize their positions or it can reduce their capacity to enter the field or to be successful. For example, within the discourses of WP, the association between parental education and the progression of children to higher education is widely documented (Brooks, 2008).

There are many species of capital at play in the field of higher education. There is the cultural capital students possess due to their parents appreciating the value of higher education and there is also the impact of economic capital. Social capital encompasses the resources that are available to the students through social networks and socially negotiated relationships that may in themselves prove beneficial, and families are often a source of social capital (Edwards, 2004). Social capital arises through social processes between the family and wider society and is composed of the many social networks that prove advantageous for the students in higher education who have it (Reay, 2000). Forms of capital are interdependent and all are ultimately rooted in economic capital. My participants spoke throughout about their financial struggles as young children and again as adults entering the field of higher education. Their lack of economic capital meant they could not enjoy the full experience of higher education as they had to work to finance themselves and support their dependants.

When Bourdieu was developing his concept of cultural capital, he engaged with the educational system at compulsory and post-compulsory levels. He argued that the students from middle-class backgrounds were more familiar with the language employed by educational institutions and therefore had an advantage over their working-class peers (Wacquant, 1998). Thus cultural capital works to the detriment of students from a working-class background as it maximizes the strategic positioning of the privileged students within the field of education. He asserted that educational institutions reinforce social inequalities and that this impacts on the way that children envisage their educational future. Therefore the less privileged carry a cumulative burden of educational disadvantage through their educational journey.

Bourdieu draws our attention to the inherent requirements of the educational system which, he asserts, 'maintain the pre-existing order, that is, the gap between pupils endowed with unequal amounts of cultural capital' (1998: 20).

This became apparent again and again in the narratives of the students in my study. In primary and secondary school they were discouraged and their potential was not tapped into because of their lack of cultural capital.

# Part Four

## Towards emancipation and empowerment

4

In this concluding section, we combine methodological, contextual, theoretical and empirical aspects of our studies and establish the links between them and the shared information. We converse about the stories of our participants that we had collected through interviews in the light of Bourdieu's *Theory of Practice*. We analysed how Bourdieu's triad can explain the continuous effort on the part of our participants because of their desire to improve their standard of living. We discuss the field and capital, habitus and symbolic violence inflicted upon the participants in our studies and the logic behind their choices. The theoretical lens of Bourdieu afforded us a fine analytical tool to go beyond the essential narrative, dig deeper and unearth and enable profound understanding of their struggles.

*Chapter 7*

# Understanding the stories from Sindh

*Ambreen Shahriar*

In this chapter, I discuss the stories of my participants collected through interviews in the light of Bourdieu's theory of practice. I analyse how Bourdieu's triad can explain the participants' persistence in their quest for a better life as a result of their desire for an improved standard of living.

## Early socialization: Field and capital

Bourdieu's concept of field, or 'field of struggles' as Jenkins (2002: 85) puts it, is a social setting that locates the agents in accordance with the significance given to their habitus and capital in that particular field. Every field identifies and approves certain capitals and rejects others. The position of an agent is identified on the basis of the already existing and known rules of the field. Families that possess a higher concentration of different types of capital transmit more capital to their children, argues Bourdieu. But the families of my participants possessed very little identifiable capital that could have given them symbolic power in that field to pass on to their children.

Finances are a major concern for people from the field to which my participants belong. Poverty was Shabana's reason for attempting suicide several times. She wanted to study but she knew that her father could not afford it because he had lost his job at the sugar mill. When asked the cause of his problems and worries, Abdur Razzak's answer was a single word that meant his whole life to him, 'poverty'. My participants realized that everything in the social world needs money, even that 'one has to have so much money to remain in contact with friends', as Shabana said. In a similar vein, 'money makes the world go around', says the musical *Cabaret*; and for Virginia Woolf 'a woman must have money and a room of her own if she is to write fiction' (*A Room of One's Own*).

The world around my participants shaped their lives – their families, relatives, neighbours and the people in their villages. What other people might say and think is more important than what they themselves (the participants) think and want. That is why there were times when it was other people who decided for them. Whenever they requested that such and such a decision should be taken about their life, the 'important others' (father, paternal uncles) did not like their interference in matters about their own lives, thus exercising symbolic power.

That's what happened to Abdur Razzak when he refused to get married because he was still going to school. 'I thought that if I were to get married, my friends would laugh at me', he said. So he decided to only get engaged. Later he indicated his wish to marry into a different family. He recalls how that wish destroyed the friendship between the two families because 'they thought that I was looking into their house' (that he was eyeing the women in their house). His father too was very upset about his son's attitude and persuaded him to marry his original fiancée. The two families did not have any contact for years, but relations have been restored recently after Abdur Razzak's father died. 'In our families, we may be very angry but when some relative passes away, then we become one all over again. In the time of sorrow, everyone comes together.'

Shabana talks about her mother, whom her family forced to marry a middle-aged man with children when she was just a young girl, even though she had received other good proposals. Shabana's father is her mother's cousin, and they married because his first wife passed away. In both these cases, 'the dominated accept as legitimate their own condition of domination' (Bourdieu and Wacquant, 1992: 167) and thus allowed the exercise of symbolic violence over them. Clearly, symbolic violence is inflicted upon my participants from members of their own families because of cultural norms that give elders power over the young. Later in this chapter, I discuss how the socially strong class inflicts symbolic violence in greater and more organized ways on people from socially weak backgrounds, like my participants.

Lareau and Horvat (1999) note that every type of capital works in its particular field so that no conclusion can be drawn without understanding and discussing the importance of the field.

## The roles and responsibilities of men and women

The roles and responsibilities of men and women in the field my participants belong to are fixed. Men are considered more powerful, and it seems that their lives are easier than women's. At the same time, men are expected to earn and provide for the whole family, and this sounds like women having the easier life. However, it is clear from the stories of my participants that just being a man or a woman does not in itself make life easy for either of them. Each gender has to perform his or her duties without fail. Their duties are different, they are expected to be different and are treated differently.

The birth of all three female participants was not welcomed by the family. However, each of them was loved dearly by their parents, especially their fathers, regardless of people 'say[ing] to my father that these are your daughters, they have to go to another house', Shabana tells us. The expectations and responsibilities of girls are similarly defined and demarcated. Farwa explains:

> Our cultural values are such that girls are brought up in such a way that they are mostly responsible by nature, this is innate in them. By responsibility I don't mean that they would take up the responsibility of the whole household; no, they would be responsible in the context of their own self, in the context of their family members. See, when in our world girls get married at a very young age, then they are responsible, they know what their responsibilities are, and what rights others have over them. What *their* rights may be is known by very few.

The attitudes and expectations of men are equally well defined. While explaining the family's reaction to his birth, Abdur Razzak says:

> They were very happy, because my father had no children from his first wife. He was nearly sixty when he had neither a son nor a daughter. Then he married for a second time, he got four daughters (before me, from my mother). He brought his brother's son up, got him an education, a job, made him a primary school teacher.

As the eldest son, Abdur Razzak has known his importance to his family all his life. He used to decide which school he would like to study in; his decision was always taken seriously. When his father asked him to leave a private school for financial reasons, and attend a government school, he went to it for a few days but didn't like it. He stubbornly refused to study at a government school and his family accepted his decision.

When his father died, Abdur Razzak's rights and duties as the eldest son changed radically. On the one hand, he gained the privilege of being head of the family – so much so that his elder sisters asked for, and followed, his advice on their affairs. On the other hand, he now shouldered the responsibility for his entire household. He said:

> That those who are younger I should get educated. I myself should work and struggle, might get a job somewhere, but their life should be comfortable, even if I am stressed. That's OK because I have already borne stress. There is one thing that the first load is the hardest to bear ... so I want that my younger siblings not to have to face problems.

The social world is subjective and objective at the same time. Despite my participants (the agents) acting and behaving in their individual ways, there are events and incidents that happen in their lives without being caused by their actions. They happen because they have to happen. In such situations the agents react in their distinctive ways. A son is the supporter of the family. Everyone looks up to him, and that is why all my participants, except Ahmar, who has an elder brother, wished they had an elder brother. Abdur Razzak, Farhana and Shabana felt deeply that if they had had an elder brother, life would have been different for them.

Even though Shabana, like Abdur Razzak, overcame this feeling of deficiency in her life and accepted responsibilities so that her younger siblings would never have to suffer, there is still an unfulfilled wish in her heart: 'If I had been a boy, I would have married someone I chose, I would have had my family settled. Now I am a girl, I can't do everything'. But Shabana is doing more than any sister or daughter in her social field could normally do. My female participants have come out of the stereotyped views of women in Pakistan and proved themselves to be active in the social world outside their homes. Yet they still feel that men have better choices and chances of surviving in the job market in Pakistani society, as I now discuss.

Beliefs such as marriage being the ultimate goal of life for a woman, or giving a dowry to girls or bride price for a girl still prevail in the social world my people belong to. More seriously, finding suitable educated men who would accept educated women as wives is difficult. This has been a problem faced by my three female participants. Shabana says, 'I could not get a proposal because I was doing a job, so people would not opt for me, [they would think] she would be the wrong type, wrong ... how can I explain that in words ... but this concept is still there.' Going out of their homes, working with men is still not considered modest in the villages of Pakistan, though things are different in the cities. At the same time, the social world is also not a safe place for these women, as they go out of their home to study and then earn. Farhana asserts that, 'people are not good.

The managers I mean ... It should not be like this that "she is a girl, we can tease her"; they should let us work independently ... I mean they would say bad things.' The other women would follow their bosses, flatter them, and so on, but Farhana was not prepared to do that. In this vein, Shabana says:

> I applied to a bank and there also I got field work, see my luck. I had to go to collect money from those people who do not pay on time, going to their houses talking to the men. I did not even have anyone from the staff with me. I did not feel secure in that job, so unfortunately I had to quit.

According to Bourdieu (1990b: 64), 'agents shape their aspirations according to the concrete indices of the accessible and the inaccessible, of what is and is not "for us", a division as fundamental and as fundamentally recognised as that between the sacred and the profane.' Each of my participants knew their boundaries and their options, especially Farhana, who could not 'go abroad to earn'. She has felt at every instance that she is a woman and therefore treated improperly, 'but they did not show [even] as much respect as should be given to a 17th grade officer, don't know why, maybe it was because we were women.'

Bourdieu (1984: 107) affirms that 'sexual properties are as inseparable from class properties as the yellowness of a lemon is from its acidity.' He states that as one moves up the social hierarchy, gender difference tends to decrease as the division of labour becomes less rigid. But here we are talking about the lowest class of society. Since my participants of both genders came from the same social class, they were expected to receive similar cultural capital, which defines the different roles and responsibilities of men and women. However, the habitus they develop is quite different, on the basis of their socialization and the views they form of the opportunity structure available to them. McClelland (1990) found through a study that men follow their habitus when they realize their professional ambitions, whereas women violate their traditional habitus when they pursue the same ambitions. Robinson and Garnier (1985) also noted that even when men and women begin their lives with similar class position and cultural capital, the social reproduction process functions in such a way that women attain less privileged positions. Therefore, social action takes place in different fields for men and for women, and men always have more symbolic power than women.

Gender is an important issue in the field my participants belong to. Both men and women have to perform their specific duties, no matter what.

Their roles and responsibilities as men and women do not give them any latitude – they are precisely defined. Responsibilities for men and women are different, and they are not easy for either group. My participants accept their roles as men and women in the particular way in which their field acknowledges them, and they agree to perform those roles. However, at the same time, they have decided to improve their and their families' social standing. But, for assuming this additional responsibility, they get no relief from their previous responsibilities, receiving little support from the people around them.

## Higher education as a key to better life

Educating their children cannot be a priority for parents when even the basic necessities of life are unavailable. The field my participants belong to assigns different roles to the two genders. It expects females to take care of their home and family and do the household chores both before and after marriage. By contrast, it expects males to earn in order to provide for the family's financial needs. Therefore, men and women have their respective duties to perform in order to make sure that life runs smoothly. Thus, for many of these poor people, educating their children is not a priority, especially when they need them for household chores or work in the fields. For them, children going to school upsets the running of their difficult lives. However, there are also poor parents who know that giving their children an education is the only way in which the family can eventually be lifted out of poverty.

The parents of both my male participants were not keen on giving them higher education. They would have preferred them to start earning in the village and support their families financially. Abdur Razzak's father certainly didn't encourage him to study. He said, 'my father wanted to stop my education then, but because of my interest he agreed to let me continue in another school.' Abdur Razzak started earning money for his family while still going to school. When he told his family that he wanted to go on to higher education, his father told him how hard up they were and asked him to decide for himself. So Abdur Razzak decided to quit university within a month of joining. His despair can be expressed through the lines of the below poem by the celebrated Urdu poet Faiz Ahmad Faiz, called '*Is waqt to yun lagta hai ab kuch bhi nhi hai*' ('Right now I feel as if there is nothing left').

| | |
|---|---|
| *Is waqt to yun lagta hai ab kuch bhi nhi hai* | Right now I feel as if there is nothing left |
| *Mahtaab na suraj, na andhera na sawera* | Neither moon, nor sun, not darkness, not dawn |
| *Ankhoan k dareechoan pe kisi husan ki chilman* | On the brink of my eyes is a glimpse of some beauty |
| *Aur dil ki panahoan main kisi dard ka dera* | And in the core of my heart is a cave filled with pain |
| *Mumkin hai koi waham tha, mumkin hai suna ho* | It is possible that what I have heard is an illusion |
| *Galyoan main kisi chaap ka ik akhri phera* | There is the last sound of some steps in the street |
| *Shakhoan main khiyaloan k ghaney pair'r ki shayad* | In the branches of the dense tree of thoughts, possibly |
| *Ab a k karey ga na koi khawab besera* | No dream will ever come and build a nest. |

A similar situation confronted Ahmar. His family problems kept him away from his studies and he had to leave and then rejoin education time and time again. However, he finally took the big step of cutting himself off from his family entirely while at university, until he had completed his degree, because he realized that the solution to his problems lay with education (on social mobility through education in France, see also Duru-Bellat, 2008).

Not only lack of economic capital (poverty) but also, even more importantly, lack of cultural capital (uneducated parents) causes families to shy away from allowing their children to be educated. None of Abdur Razzak's close family members had gone into higher education, so no cultural capital could be passed on to the younger members of the extended family – which is why Abdur Razzak quit university within a month of starting. Likewise, Ahmar lived in an extended family where his uncles and his father's uncles all disliked his and his brothers' efforts to obtain an education and made every effort to undermine their efforts to study. That 'families are corporate bodies animated by ... a tendency to perpetuate their social being, with all its powers and privileges, which is at the basis of *reproduction strategies*' (Bourdieu, 1998: 19, original emphasis), caused problems for my participants.

Some examples show that cultural capital in the form of education passed on in earlier generations makes it more likely that the parents favour educating their children, and this willingness is even more important than having the money to pay for it. Only someone who badly wants something will make the effort to obtain the necessary resources.

In the case of Ahmar's family, his mother insisted that her sons be educated, and his father was also educated and was in a government job. But his other relatives thought differently. They saw education as a threat and feared that their children would also demand it. This illustrates the way uneducated relatives try to hinder the education of the educated branch of their extended family. By contrast, Farwa was an example of how the educated members of a family can 'convert' the uneducated ones. Farwa's mother was educated and wanted her children to be too. Through the close interactions in an extended family, she could influence the other mothers too, so that other girls in the family were also educated. In Farwa's family, unlike Ahmar's, boys were already being educated. According to Bourdieu (1977), the habitus of an agent generates such strategies, which are aimed at 'the preservation or improvement of their positions with respect to the defining capital of the field' (Jenkins, 2002: 85). Thus, Farwa's family already possesses capital – educating boys – and they aimed to improve their position in the field by educating their girls as well; whereas Ahmar's family did not possess any such capital and therefore resisted it in order to preserve their position in the field.

It seems that when mothers are educated, they are able to transfer this capital to their daughters, as in the case of all three of my women participants (see Reay, 2000; Stevenson and Baker, 1987; Bogenschneider, 1997). They regard education as a weapon that would help their daughters fight the vicissitudes of life.

Shabana's story illustrates this. She had a *nikah* with her husband when she was only a few days old. *Rukhsati* (the ceremony of sending the bride to the groom's house to live there with him) never happened. Problems arose when Shabana wanted to study. Her in-laws wanted the *rukhsati* to take place, so that Shabana would go to their house and live with them. But Shabana's parents made it clear that they wanted their children to study and they would not do Shabana's *rukhsati* since she was only a teenager at that time.

Shabana explains:

> My maternal family was educated, my uncles used to get their daughters educated so my mother had this interest in getting her daughter [Shabana] educated. She said that [her] children [Shabana and her siblings] should also study. My mother wanted that the problems she faced should not be faced by her children.

Not only do such educated mothers think, but they are actually able to develop more favourable conditions for female education in the field. The children develop a habitus that understands the importance of education. Farwa recalls: 'I had seen members of my family ... always busy reading, I saw my mother, my father, my sister, who was a poet. They used to write, they used to read. I did not like that.' But then Farwa started reading and gradually developed an interest. Therefore the capital owned and the habitus developed at home eventually resulted in her obtaining a PhD. By contrast, the mothers of both male participants are illiterate, which meant that their sisters were uneducated as well.

Generally, my participants see education for the two genders differently. The education of girls is always less important than the education of boys. Shabana decided to give up the thought of doing an MPhil because the money it costs would be enough for the education of two of her brothers, which she thought to be more important. Neither of the male participants considers female education a priority. Therefore, when it comes to getting education, what matters is cultural capital and not economic capital. It seems that, in the case of my participants from economically poor families, cultural capital can work without the support of economic capital (see for instance Reay, 2004). However, lack of economic capital meant that my participants had to struggle and face great hardships, but they were ready to bear this pain to get (higher) education. Bourdieu explained school success by the amount and type of cultural capital inherited from the family milieu rather than by measures of individual talent or achievement (Reay, 2004). Therefore, in order to implement Bourdieu's model of practice in the educational field, it is important to consider both capital owned and habitus developed. These students in Sindh show that cultural capital plays a significant role in the parents' decision to educate their children. However, it does not seem to affect achievement in their case, since they struggled to gain education because of their personal interest and their experiences during early and later socialization (see also Dumais, 2002). The early socialization of a child in the field develops habitus, due to acquisition of capital and a response to that.

## Habitus developed through time

Habitus is primarily 'one's view of the world and one's place in it' (Dumais, 2002: 45). Habitus can manifest as 'the language use, skills, orientations, attitudes, dispositions, and schemes of perception that children are endowed with by virtue of socialization in their families and communities' (Lin, 1999: 407). Habitus, as I've used it, is a subjective but not an individual system of internalized structures. Bourdieu (1977) argues, and I agree, that being a product of chronological experiences, dominated by the early life experiences that continue to structure and restructure it, habitus continues from restructuring to further restructuring. Therefore, whenever an agent moves to a new social structure with different recognized capitals, the habitus builds upon new structures and understandings of the field. Agreeing with Bourdieu, I found that the habitus of my participants developed mostly from the interactions in the family and in the village during childhood and adolescence. As the person makes further contact with the world and moves to a different environment, they shift away from the initial habitus and adapt to a new field.

The five young men and women in this study possessed different quantities of the various forms of capital and these affected their attitudes and reactions to the world and life in general. Their possession of certain types of capital allowed them certain choices; others were denied them because of the capital they did not possess. Seen as from another perspective, the types of capital they did possess limited their choices, since a choice that suits one type of capital might not suit another (see Reay, 1995a). Moreover the kind of capital in their possession and its quantity positioned each agent in the force field – as Swartz (1997: 73–4) sees it, 'they become objects of struggle as valued resources'.

These students formed their habitus through their particular socialization within the family and their encounters with the outside world, typically in the village. Each had to face restrictions, boundaries and limitations imposed mostly by their parents. Sometimes the boundaries were of gender, as in the case of those who were forbidden to do certain things because they were girls. For others, the boundaries were those of age, as in the case of Abdur Razzak, who was not allowed to go out of the house on his own to play with other children. He only understood the reasons for these restrictions much later. He says:

> Children used to go to filthy water, we were kids. There are many muddy fields and irrigation and sewerage ditches, as it is a *kacho* [rural] area, so we might fall. We were mischievous and could fall from heights etc., so they [parents] were worried ... about death even. They were careful and did not want me to be hurt. One gets hurt by playing in shrubs; there are thorns.

The worst thing for little Abdur Razzak was that other children in his village who did not study were allowed to have fun in the mud. He not only had to go to school but was also forbidden from playing in the neighbourhood. There are fascinating parallels between the situation of Abdur Razzak, who was not allowed to play with the ordinary children in his village, and the cautionary tale of the little German boy who was told by his supercilious parents 'not to play with the rabble-children' ('*Spiel nicht mit den Schmuddelkindern*'; Franz-Josef Degenhardt, 1965). From the beginning, he was told that he was different from other children, children who play in filthy water and do not go to school. This attitude of parents was also expressed by Ahmar, who noticed while still a child that he and his brother were different from the other children at school (see Shariar, 2013a). Abdur Razzak was told that he had to study and this proved very important later in his life. Later, he understood the importance of education and knew it to be the only solution to his family's financial problems.

By contrast, Farhana didn't listen to her mother about not playing in the neighbourhood but followed her whim. Though in time her whims led her in a different direction. She explains, 'when I used to get scolded on going out, then in sorrow I would recite the Qur'an, read its explanations, I got more inclined towards it then.' And soon Farhana understood her mother's principles too:

> My mother was like this: she would not want us to go out a lot, girls should not roam around. Like, they are simple people who want their daughters to be respectable. They don't want to let us live as it is, she wanted us to spend life in an honourable way. She would never tell us to put on make-up or get a haircut. She never told us to change ourselves, she let us be the way we were [simple].

During Farhana's childhood and teenage years her mother's attitudes – that she must grow up specifically as a *simple* girl, whereas she wanted her mother to tell her about putting on make-up – left a mark on Farhana's life. She could not be settled with her classmates and colleagues from the city at university and when she had a job. She found that she was different from them in many ways.

Farwa, however, remained determined and assertive. She was a natural rebel. She did what she thought right, not what she was told, even by her mother. Her attitudes were encouraged and discouraged at the same time. On the one hand, her mother gave her a good hiding from time to time when she had overstepped the mark. On the other hand, she knew that her father and many male members of the family admired her tomboy behaviour. This approval by at least some of her family helped her later in life and enabled her to pursue her interests in spite of the many obstacles she had to overcome.

Although Ahmar's childhood is completely different, the role of parental attitudes and expectations can be noticed in his case too. From a young age he was responsible for everything; he and his brothers helped his father to build their brick house. He used to work in the fields and, he says, 'when the flowering season for cotton arrived, we used to collect it and sell a kilo or so to buy our books, and that would be it.' He never questioned this, as his father was too busy with his job to notice. His mother approved because she knew that her sons wanted the money for their education and that they wouldn't waste money on idle amusements. And, indeed, they never did. Dumais (2002: 46) suggests 'by internalizing the social structure and one's place in it, one comes to determine what is possible and what is not possible for one's life and develops aspirations and practices accordingly.' Thus, all my participants draw upon the actions and attitudes of their parents towards them while positioning themselves, and they all continue from there in their personal lives as well, when they have to make their own decisions.

All three women said that their fathers love them dearly. Their mothers were from socially higher families than their fathers. And their mothers were all educated, Farhana said:

> My mother's family ... she is Qureshi. That family is also educated. My mother studied till 5th grade. Her father was a *Sahib* [*Sahibs* are external inspectors at primary and secondary levels in village schools]; there used to be *Sahibs* in those days. My grandmother is also literate; my maternal uncles [mother's brothers] are also educated. One of my uncles was a director, director in sports. He has retired now. The other one works on the railways and another works in education.

Shabana said that her parents would not take them to weddings and other gatherings in the village, believing that that would disturb their education. Even when Shabana was ill, her father didn't allow her to skip school. 'In his opinion, if a child misses school once, it can easily become a habit.' Her teachers used to praise her example to other children. Thus the significance of education was an important capital transmitted at an early age to my participants, both female and male, although family support for continued education varied later on.

My participants developed their habitus through early socialization at home and in the village, and it continued to develop throughout their lives as socialization increased. But the attitudes and expectations of parents and relatives during early life had the greatest impact.

This bears out a saying attributed to St Ignatius of Loyola (1491–1556), founder of the Roman Catholic order of the Jesuits: 'Give me a child until he is seven and I will give you the man.' The Jesuits believed that the years from one to seven are the most formative years, and they largely determine the character (habitus) of the adult.

However, when the habitus encounters an unknown field, the agents find themselves disconnected and in a vacuum. And in such situations my participants showed strength and courage, like Sassui, the famous heroine of Sindhi folklore (Sur Sassui). They decided not to give up their struggle in the face of hardship. Shah Abdul Latif Bhittai (1689–1752) expresses it like this:

| | |
|---|---|
| *Tatti Thadhi Kaah, Kanhain Weil Wehanrh Ji* | Whether hot or cold, march on, there is no time to rest |
| *Mataan Thay Oondah, Per Na Laheen Pireen Jo* | Lest darkness falls and you fail to find your destination. |

They then transform themselves and adapt as soon as possible to the requirements of the new field. This gives them a deeper understanding of the power relations and their own position in the field of power. When my participants moved from their home setting to university, they faced symbolic violence, resulting from the disjuncture.

## Symbolic violence

My participants all plan to make a place for themselves in the existing social structure through higher education. Due to their particular cultural capital, they didn't bring the kind of habitus needed with them to the city. They had the right attitudes and were very keen on gaining education but they were lacking in language skills and confidence to take part actively in university life (see also Lin, 1999).

The capital owned and the habitus formed from early socialization onwards determine the strategies that agents implement in the field. In the field of education, the strategies activated by the parents of each of the five students included their insistence on education and curbing all the activities that could prove to be hindrances to early education. So they appreciated the value of education and made persistent efforts to pursue it. However, to have more possibilities at hand and generate effective strategies to continue their education they needed more relevant capital. Because they lacked the right kind of capital for what they wanted to achieve, they faced problems.

These students felt themselves to be different from others because of their appearance or social standing. When Ahmar joined a college in the nearby city, he and other friends from his village felt embarrassed because they used to wear *shalwar kameez* (traditional Indian dress), while the other boys were in trousers and shirts. Not just their Western clothes but their coming from English-medium schools made Ahmar feel inferior. Similarly when Shabana joined university, her uncle told her:

> Some people will come in Mitsubishi Pajeros, some will come in other big cars, some will have fathers who are professors there ... but you don't have to wish the same for your father. Just think of your studies, you don't have to pay any attention to all those cars and that show-off stuff.

When Shabana was at university, she noticed that 'everyone was from good families economically and socially, it was just me who was from a poor family. But even then, I never let them feel that I am a villager or that I am poor.' This gave rise to 'split habitus' (Bourdieu, 2003). Bourdieu's humble family and his elite school developed split habitus and made a critic out of him, allowing him to write from experience about the injustices in society. In a similar way, Shabana behaved differently in front of her university friends and her friends in the village. Farwa also reported doing the same.

The notion of habitus helped to expose the relationships of my participants and others from their background to the dominant culture. Wherever they went they carried their cultural capital with them. This limited their choices. Bourdieu's concept of symbolic violence helps us to understand their resulting 'misery of position' (Bourdieu, 1993). By accepting the rules made by the dominant class, the dominated class accepts that dominance. By participating in the social order as it is, the dominated recognize that 'they are beaten before they begin' (Bourdieu, 1984: 165). However, no other choice is available: they have to participate whether they like it or not.

Bourdieu (1986: 244) states that, 'the scholastic yield from educational action depends on the cultural capital previously invested by the family' and on the '*type* and *prestige* of the educational institution attended' (Swartz, 1997: 193, original emphasis). According to Bourdieu's theory of social reproduction and cultural capital, the culture transmitted by the dominant class is supported by the educational system (Bourdieu and Passeron, 1977). This, in turn, means that members of the dominated class can never compete on an equal footing with those of the dominant class, as their habitus is incompatible with that expected in school. Therefore, the dominated and the dominant 'do not compete from equal starting points; thus social stratification is reproduced' (Lin, 1999: 394).

In the social hierarchy, all are competing in the same job market. It identifies and acknowledges the capital owned by the privileged class, since the rules of society are laid down by this class. All parties (teachers, students, curriculum designers, parents, job seekers, organizations, their selection boards and bosses) by and large take these rules for granted and consider them legitimate. This is an example of symbolic violence inflicted on the dominated class in general and on my participants in particular. My participants dealt with this symbolic violence by acquiring more symbolic capital, thus transforming their habitus and making it more useful in the new field.

## Logic of practice

People inherit their social class (Sayer, 2005), but it determines their personal, social, cultural and economic ranking. The social, cultural, linguistic and academic capital my participants inherited had no symbolic value. They are aware of their disadvantaged and dominated position and want to move up the social strata. Through 'new creative responses' (Reay 1995a: 356) to the changing social field, they created a habitus that helped them to survive.

Choice is at the heart of habitus. But by default each habitus offers only a finite number of choices. That is why my participants had to develop their own ways of progressing through life. Abdur Razzak, for instance, chose his schools, made his own decisions and acted like a free agent except when circumstances forced him to leave university. On that occasion, he had no choice, at least in his mind, but to renounce higher education and rejoin his family, which needed his support. He followed the current and flow of life as it came to him. Ahmar, by contrast, gave up contact with everyone at home. Shabana continued to be herself regardless of her social class. She mingled with other girls and made lots of friends, though with a split habitus (behaving differently in her different environments). A striking example of a British Muslim woman living with a split habitus is depicted in the 2004 Channel 4 film *Yasmin*, directed by Kenneth Glenaan. Unlike Shabana, Farhana preferred her own shell. However, their starting situation was not the same. Bourdieu (1981) discusses the adjustment made by agents between their 'subjective vocations', that is, what they want to do, and their 'objective missions' – what they are expected to do. They combine the two modes of behaviour, choosing the former when they can but obeying the latter when they have to. Therefore, in terms of Bourdieu (1990a), their habitus tends to produce acceptable behaviours in keeping with their capital and field and to eliminate all the behaviours that are incompatible with them. Thus 'practice has a logic which is not that of the logician. This has to be acknowledged in order to avoid asking of it more logic than it can give' (Bourdieu, 1990a: 86).

At other times, my participants enjoyed moments of activation of their capital. Abdur Razzak activated his social capital and got help from the principal of the school where he studied. Ahmar gave tuition while being a student at the same tuition centre, activating his educational capital. Shabana made use of her habitus, her good nature, in settling down when she came to university. 'I make friends very easily with everyone. I am liked very much by all, given a lot of love. I don't know whether it's due to my pleasant behaviour or theirs. But I make friends very easily even with passers-by in the street,' explained Shabana. Lareau and Horvat (1999: 39) stress that 'to be of value in a given field, social and cultural capital must be activated.'

Another way of adapting to habitus is apparent, especially in Farwa and Farhana. When they arrived at the University of Sindh, each realized that, in Farhana's words, 'there is a lot of difference between the environment of the village and of the city. The village girls and the city girls are very different.' Farhana was uncomfortable at university: 'I used to feel a little uneasy. Our social setup was completely different and in the city the girls are of another type, they are different. I used to stay quiet, would not mingle much.' In her discomfort, Farhana adjusted her habitus by being quiet, as she realized that she could not socialize with the women at the university. Unlike Farhana, Shabana and Farwa made themselves at home there and made some friends. Farwa had to become less assertive and stubborn in order to adapt her habitus to the new field. She said:

> When you are at home, you can do anything, your family will forgive you, owns you, but outside home it is not like that. There is always a punishment ready for whatever you do wrong [against the accepted ways/norms]. So this brought changes to my personality. After that, the aggressiveness of my personality, lack of self-control, the feelings of inadequacy ... I took control of that myself and all these factors were responsible, the whole context helped me towards it [calming her aggressive nature].

My participants came from a disadvantaged socio-economic background, so their habitus did not equip them with the skills and confidence they needed to cope with the modern urban world. But, unlike their counterparts who gave up in the face of adversity, they transformed their habitus through a 'creative discursive agency'. Flowerdew and Miller (2008: 203) define creative discursive agency as 'how individuals are able to initiate or take advantage of opportunities for the creative development of their discursive practices.' My participants are cast in a reactive role, owing to the power of social structure: class condition, capital composition and habitus making them unable to initiate positive action, some of them utilize their creative discursive agency in order to counterbalance the weight of social structure (for a supporting argument, see Collins, 1993). Ahmar and Farwa developed creative discursive agency to cope with issues of confidence, language skills and, most importantly, appearance and style. Through creative discursive agency both responded interactively to the demands of the social field and finally made a better position for themselves in society.

These students were ready for the transmutation of their habitus, triggered by some personal or collective predicament in their lives. Ahmar knew about the quarrels in the village and when he was slapped by a policeman, he resolved to become an officer in the armed forces himself.

Farwa knew that everyone in the family except her was fond of studying, but that was not enough to induce her to study in earnest. Several events moved her to change her habitus and study vigorously. First she won a speech competition at school and received lavish praise. Later her elder sister began to study medicine and thereby set an example. Thus encouraged, she threw herself into her studies and now has a PhD and is an assistant professor of psychology.

Shabana decided to get divorced and, after overcoming various obstacles, succeeded. Now becoming educated was her only way to regain respectability and to prove herself.

The habitus of Ahmar, Farwa and Shabana allowed individual agency and when they applied it, they succeeded in transmuting their habitus. Abdur Razzak's habitus was deeply influenced by bigger social structures and therefore did not allow him enough agency to do this. What made him give up on the studies he started were the demands and values of his old habitus, his concerns not only about the poverty of his family but even more for their safety, since they lived close to an area overrun by dacoits, thieves and bandits, where the women and children of the family needed the protection of a young man. Abdur Razzak's father asked him to give up his education for the sake of his family but didn't force him to do so; Abdur Razzak made his own decision. We see that 'while the habitus allows for individual agency it also predisposes individuals towards certain ways of behaving' (Reay, 1995b: 354–5).

My participants were trying to activate their capital and transform their habitus in order to gain access to education and thereby to prestigious jobs. In spite of all these creative efforts, all were constrained by the limited choices available to them for connecting with their new environment. In spite of their limited capital and their consequent limited choices, they were able to transform their attitudes, dispositions, skills and self-image – that is, their habitus and social view. My observations confirm Collins's (1993) view that individual creative, discursive agency (including activation, negation and transformation of habitus) can be effective – though not always possible – in coping with one's social world, despite the larger constraining, reproducing social structures outlined by Bourdieu (1977).

*Chapter 8*

# Interpreting the stories from rural Ireland

*Teresa Bruen*

> *Let us go forth, the tellers of tales, and seize whatever prey the heart longs for, and have no fear. Everything exists, everything is true, and the earth is only a little dust under our feet.*
>
> William Butler Yeats (1865–1939)

I have employed the theoretical lens of Bourdieu to interpret the findings of my enquiry. He suggested that the role of social science was to comprehend how objective structures of society such as social roles, norms and institutions influence subjective behaviour and then how the entirety of social behaviour enables the reproduction of the reality that is society (Fries, 2009). To achieve a comprehensive understanding of the mature student experiences, I engage Bourdieu's conceptual thinking tools: habitus, capital and field. These concepts have been utilized as analytical tools within the field of educational research as a means to comprehend the social and cultural processes that have a propensity to ensure the reproduction of social inequalities (Fleming and Finnegan, 2011). Bourdieu suggests that these concepts are interdependent: none of them is primary. The concept of habitus, deployed alongside capital, and the manner in which they function in particular fields, present tools for comprehending the continuing impact of social inequality on mature students' lives (Fleming and Finnegan, 2011).

I use direct quotes to ensure that the reader gets a sense of their feelings and experiences. From the beginning of my study I had strongly believed that the voices of these mature students should be at the forefront of this enquiry. During the analysis of the data there were some 'aha' moments of comprehension for myself and the students, who would say, 'I never thought about this before.' This comment was made in relation to their experiences of education throughout their lives. A sense of understanding emerged as themes were developed. The students were asked: 'Would you like to tell me about your experiences of education to date?' This chapter amalgamates the findings garnered through this question. They began from their earliest experiences of compulsory education through to present-day experiences of higher education. There is no hierarchy in the order of the main themes and sub-themes; they are simply presented in the order they arose within the narrative (Table 8.1).

**Table 8.1:** Main themes and sub-themes

| Main themes | Sub-themes |
|---|---|
| 1. Experiences of first- and second-level education | Negative experiences at primary and secondary level.<br>Streaming on entry to secondary school.<br>Relationships with teachers.<br>Home background.<br>Impact of support classes.<br>Struggle. |
| 2. Family support | The culture of education within the family.<br>Farming community: work on the farm was prioritized. |
| 3. Going to college | Reasons and motivations for returning to education.<br>Sense of fear.<br>Selection of college. |
| 4. Balancing study and work and family commitments | Constantly prioritizing duties.<br>Attendance. |
| 5. Supportive networks | Support at home.<br>Support staff within the college.<br>Importance of friends. |
| 6. Pleasant surprise | Enjoyment of higher education.<br>Increased self-worth.<br>Lecturers' style and influence. |

## Habitus

I use the concept of habitus in relation to the analysis of themes and sub-themes to gain deeper understanding of the students' stories. Habitus refers to values, expectations and lifestyles of social groups gained through the experiences in their everyday lives and which become their dispositions. 'Experiences of first- and second-level education' was a core theme of discussion. They reported having negative experiences of compulsory education at both primary and secondary level and of feeling despair, frustration, disappointment, conveyed through their body language and tone of voice as well as their words. Their habitus certainly influenced their experiences of education at all levels, as was evident in their comments about education.

Geraldine, who was in residential care from an early age, said:

> That was the way life was. I done my junior cert' and it was quite funny, well not funny that my principal at the time because I had been in care, that negativity from being in care went with me into secondary school.

Habitus encompasses ways of behaving and socially learnt dispositions that are at times taken for granted and are attained throughout the course of everyday life. These lasting behaviours are learnt throughout childhood and generally reflect the social context through which they were obtained (Fleming and Finnegan, 2011). Habitus helps us to understand the 'relationships with teachers' identified as a sub-theme and allows for appreciation of structures and cultures of schools and institutes the mature students engaged with. Through habitus we can comprehend the context for behaviours and actions that led to negative experiences.

Kenneth talked about his relationship with teachers and how he found himself bored and unstimulated in class. He was placed in a low-rated class, not because of his academic ability but because of his socio-economic background:

> We all ended up in C, you know, so when you look back on it what are the chances? I didn't mind the class but the way I would look at it is the best way to keep a child's interest is to keep them sorta challenged. If they find it too easy you've lost it.

Their habitus did not fit with the culture of their schools, nor within the field of education. My findings suggest that this led to the students feeling that they didn't belong. As Wright (2011) has highlighted, rigid adherence to procedures and lack of imagination are demonstrated by teachers who fail to explore the reasons why students behave in a certain way. Joseph spoke about how for him and his mother, who was a single parent in Catholic Ireland, the religious domination of schools was itself a challenge. But there was never any understanding by the religious order as to why he behaved as he did; it was never acknowledged that their treatment and lack of understanding in relation to his family background precipitated his behaviour.

> Primary school definitely didn't go well with me – my mother was a single mother when we first went in, and the school was run by nuns so she was blacklisted really they didn't talk to her.

Habitus persuades us to consider in relational terms rather than in opposites. Therefore the relationship between teachers and the structures of the organization had significant outstanding effects. The mature students' habitus was structured through their past and present experiences and shaped their practices and behaviours. Habitus works relationally with one's present circumstances. The teachers had little understanding of the personal habitus of them as children and this led to behaviours that reproduced social inequality within the educational system, creating poor relationships with their teachers. This impacted negatively on the students' school experiences. Grenfell (2004) reasons that poor relationships with teachers arise when students are put in their place by things that happen in the classroom. They happen, he suggests, because of students' lack of connection with the educational system and the teachers' disconnection with their personal habitus. It may happen by stealth in thousands of tiny interactions. The students talked of the subtle and some not-so-subtle behaviours of their teachers that made them feel excluded, so they didn't attain their potential. The students recounted interactions with teachers who implied that they did not fit and wouldn't succeed. Some of these students had undiagnosed learning difficulties that the teachers mistook for laziness. Teachers were wholly unaware of these students' cognitive habitus and this made for difficult relationships.

Joseph said:

> When I first went to primary school I was diagnosed, well the teachers told me that I was dyslexic. But that was when I was about five, but the other teacher told my mother that I was just lazy and that went on until I was 12.

Three of these students were treated by some of their teachers in ways that by today's standards would constitute bullying. Negative experiences of schooling have a lasting effect (Wright, 2011) and this was evident when the students recounted their negative experiences, even though it all happened a good many years ago. They talked about how the impact of these experiences reverberated right through to their adult lives, and especially affected their decision making about entering higher education. Habitus as a concept permits us to understand this powerful effect as it is robust, long-lasting and transposable, becoming active in a diverse array of theatres of social action (Bourdieu, 1993).

Bourdieu emphasizes the collective nature of educational disadvantage and the critical significance of a child's early experiences of school. Reay (2002) examined the transition of mature students to higher education and found that they had 'troubled educational histories', but she highlights narratives of educational survival and recovery. We see this too in the narratives of the mature students. Their stories demonstrate tenacity, resilience and ambition to succeed in spite of their earlier troubled experiences. Previous research found that students from disadvantaged social backgrounds developed coping strategies that were useful in helping them succeed in higher education. Habitus enables us to understand this, as its influence is progressed largely through imitation. People unconsciously copy and integrate behaviours they have seen in their social world into their own lives. Mature students who survived past negative experiences were adaptable enough on entering higher education to observe the behaviours of the prevailing group and integrate them into their own lives.

One of the motivations for entering higher education was to acquire a qualification to achieve better employment or progress through their chosen field of expertise.

Noreen spoke about her ambitions:

> I thought about it for a few years going back and genuinely I didn't think I had the ability to do it. That was number one, and I was constantly questioning. I didn't do well in secondary school, what makes me think that I can now go on and do this? lot of places required that you have qualifications. So that was what started me and I thought well I'll just start on simple little things. So I went back and I started doing courses and I got a job.

She went on to talk about the notion of gaining a third-level qualification:

> So I needed a qualification that was going to allow me to go out and do further things, bigger things if you like, different things for want of a better word and not I suppose restrict myself to childcare.

Due to their lack of educational qualifications, most of the mature students had spent their lives in unskilled occupations. Willis (1978) proposed in his ethnographic study that working-class kids tended to get working-class jobs and asked why middle-class children get middle-class jobs and why the others let them. And he questioned how working-class kids get working-class jobs and why they allow it. The analytical tool of habitus helps to resolve this complex issue as it centres on the way people act, think and feel. It encompasses our histories and demonstrates how we bring our history into our current circumstances and how we then make choices to behave in a certain manner. Our past experiences shape the vision of our future. Some choices may not seem possible to us because of our past (Maton, 2008).

Joseph said:

> I was in rehab for a drink problem and I done out a list of what I wanted to do and that was the last thing on the list that I wanted to do and so I turned around and done it and eventually it took me a while, but I don't think that I was actually ready to do it until I went back.

He said that the possibility of a good job motivated him to return to education:

> To be honest the motivation is I don't want to sound fickle I would like to get offered jobs that instead of having to use my body I'd have to use my mind. I would prefer not to have to scrape together €600 so I can go and see my sister with my girlfriend and have to go and kip in my aunt's house. I don't want anything like that. I want to be able to say, 'Oh yeh there's a concert.' I want to be able to afford that this week instead of having to wait a month and then say 'Can I afford the ticket?' and that's one of the biggest motivations and that's always at the back of my head.

Geraldine told us about her motivation for going to college, which came to her when she was homeless and living on the streets. She recalled a powerful memory:

> I used to go and sit down by the Four Courts all day as it was somewhere that was dry. Even at that age, I used to listen to so many people coming up before a judge, and the solicitors representing them used to say 'He left school at an early age' and it seemed to be a repeat thing for so many people who were up in front of a judge. It was the one big thing, the defence that they all seemed to have in common, and I thought that was odd even at the age of 15. I thought I don't want to turn out like this.

The relationship between habitus and a person's social world can be mismatched, as habitus can generate practices long after the original conditions that shaped them have disappeared. This was challenging for these students as they brought with them behaviours and actions arising out of their earlier educational experiences. Grenfell (2004) suggests that many students are excluded from education because the way education is presented to them doesn't fit their cognitive habitus, so they talk of feeling like a fish out of water. Maton (2008: 59) explains:

> As 'fish in water', social agents are typically unaware of the supporting, life-affirming water, the match between their habituses and the fields in which they flourish or feel ill at ease, and how they come to be in these contexts.

The first year of higher education was especially difficult. The disconnection between their personal cognitive habitus and the institutional habitus influenced their experiences. As Kenneth said of the first year:

> But like the whole experience of coming into like third level for a good while of it I would have been sort of like a deer in the headlights, do you know what I mean like? Really when I look back on it especially the first up until Christmas, but maybe a bit after it all of that is sort of a blur [laughs].

They expressed the unease and fear they felt in the first year, which they found difficult to adjust to. This was because of the mismatch between their personal and cognitive habitus and the institutional habitus of the field of higher education.

## Capital

Bourdieu's concept of capital was a useful tool for understanding the narratives of the mature students. Bourdieu suggested that there are four main forms of capital: economic, related to finances and assets; cultural, which incorporates knowledge, taste, language and voice; social capital, encompassing networks, family, religious and cultural heritage; and symbolic capital, which involves all other forms of capital that can be exchanged within other fields. Most powerful is economic capital (Moore, 2008). These students were economically disadvantaged and this impacted their studies. The amount of capital that an individual brings to a field endows them with an advantage and enables them to be more competitive. Broadly, capital comprises the resources people have access to that can advantage them within a given field. The lack of cultural capital in relation to the field of compulsory education is implied in their narratives to be a reason for their unease and fear of the field of higher education. Mills and Gale (2007) suggest that the cultural capital of marginalized groups is not valued in an equitable way by the educational system. The students spoke about how they were poorly treated and discriminated against on account of their 'home background'. Geraldine talked about the negative impact her home background had for her. She was in care from an early age and was currently homeless. She identifies her lack of cultural capital thus:

> Even going to friends' houses after school and you'd see the parents go 'now homework time', and you would actually see the mother and father sitting down, taking the time and this is the way we do it. It was interesting even as a kid looking at how they were and it was interaction with their kids, time for some one on one.

Capital was inherent in the theme of 'relationships with teachers'. The teachers' opinions of their family background and undiagnosed learning difficulties created challenging relationships that affected their experiences. Fleming and Finnegan (2010) suggest that mature students linked the manner in which they were treated with disrespect, and the low expectations of their academic ability to the fact that they did not come from a privileged background. Many of the students felt they were treated differently because of their social standing or family background, which I have identified as a sub-theme: 'the culture of education within the family'. The students' lack of relevant capital was consistently expressed. There is almost a fatalistic notion at work here: they were doomed to fail through their lack of capital. As Henry et al. (1998: 142) observe: 'The school assumes middle-class culture, attitudes and values in all its pupils. Any other background however rich in experiences, often turns out to be a liability.'

Their culture and values were not valued within the compulsory educational sector and in fact disadvantaged this cohort of students. Geraldine reflected on her experiences:

> It was like, oh you're a troublesome child because social workers were involved and I was stigmatised because of that by the teachers as well. I had an awful lot of trouble I suppose with the teachers because of it. It was anytime that there was something wrong it was my fault I was there, because I was the one that didn't have the parent and you're a troublesome child and that's the end of it and nobody wants you.

I found listening to this difficult and moving.

Bourdieu (1997) argues that, to succeed, children need to be furnished with a range of cultural behaviours. Privileged children and, significantly, their teachers, have learnt these behaviours, whereas unprivileged children have not. The mature students did not have the customary cultural capital to succeed in the educational sector and this explains the behaviour of the teachers and how the mature students found their experiences at the HEI so difficult.

Bourdieu (1997) proposes that educational institutes reinforce social inequalities through not understanding the amounts of cultural capital the students possess. The mature students didn't have the opportunity to amass the cultural capital that would advantage them because of academic streaming at school. Being kept in the lowest stream prevented exposure to the dominant group, which could have helped them acquire cultural capital. Ivan summed up how he felt about academic streaming:

> You find a comfort in it but there's nothing to say that do you know if you were with people who were brighter than you or more cleverer than you in the first place that you wouldn't strive or that if you were friends with them it might rub off on you a bit more, I don't know to be honest.

Being blocked from acquiring cultural capital persisted when they embarked on higher education. They had little opportunity to avail themselves of extracurricular activities because of their other commitments. Opportunities to socialize with students from different backgrounds were limited and so could not amass relevant cultural and social capital by learning from the dominant class.

Cultural capital within the family network of the mature students was particularly significant. Education had not been prioritized especially for those from a farming background. Ivan, Noreen and Kenneth all stressed how greatly farm work was prioritized. The families were poor, from a rural background where the small farm was their only source of income.

Noreen said:

> There was a serious amount of work to get through in the morning before I got to school ... what happened in the evening was the farm work took over so there wasn't the time to apply myself to the books and the homework and forget the studies they didn't even exist and I suppose there wasn't the support at

> home to do the study and if I had more time it might have been different, but my time you know it just wasn't there.

There is a long-standing connection between parental education and children's progression to higher education. The literature suggests that progression to higher education is still uncommon for people from a working-class background (Brooks, 2003). When speaking about family support in relation to early educational experiences they were talking about parents, siblings and, in one case, foster parents and staff at a residential home. Capital allows for the analysis of the significance of support for students but these mature students had acquired no cultural capital in relation to education within their families. Mills and Gale (2007) suggested that time in school was an extravagance for many poor students. Wright (2011) describes the working-class expectation that one should become economically independent on reaching the minimum school leaving age and that to have more than a minimum education is seen as a luxury. Certainly the families of these students did not expect them to continue their education beyond the minimum basic requirement.

Cultural capital has been employed through Bourdieu's work as a means to illuminate the relationship between scholastic achievement with the irregular allocation of dispositions, understandings and abilities that were typically conveyed through families. Bourdieu (1986) suggests that families could advance these qualities by transmitting their cultural capital in three ways: through an embodied state encompassing cultural tastes; in an objectified state; in the shape of cultural goods such as books; or in an institutionalized structure, as in educational qualifications. The families of the mature participants did not have access to these forms of cultural capital and so they were unable to develop the qualities that would have allowed the individuals to achieve academic success (Fleming and Finnegan, 2011).

Bourdieu and Passerson (1977) suggest that children from wealthier backgrounds inherit forms of capital that make it easier for them to progress within the academic field. They propose that children who have inherited appropriate cultural capital speak the same language as their teachers and are believed to be brighter than children who do not have these advantages. It has also been suggested that valued cultural knowledge is acquired in the home.

An interesting theme throughout their narratives was how they came to decide to enter higher education. The decision-making process was to them significant and they identified it as a main theme of 'going to college'. Their past educational experiences played a significant part in their decision. Wright (2011) suggested that mature students made connections across time, examining past educational experiences and finding them to be significant for their expectations for higher education.

These students were dubious about entering higher education because of their past sense of failure. Their motivations were set against a backdrop of educational failure and so their decision was all the more courageous. They had moments of self-doubt about their academic abilities and what would be expected of them. Bourdieu describes this as a feeling of not knowing the rules of the game, making their transition to higher education challenging. They are playing a game of catch-up with peers who have relevant cultural capital at their disposal. They had little knowledge of the expectations and the organizational structure of the field of higher education and this led to a 'sense of fear'. This is especially true for mature students, who were the first generation of their families to enter higher education, so they could only relate to their past educational experiences. It is their lack of cultural capital that explains the origins of their fears and uncertainties. Fleming and Finnegan (2011) suggested that mature students remained uncertain of their ability to cope with the academic demands of higher education and this lack of confidence is wholly due to the legacy of previous negative experiences. Bourdieu and Passeron (1977) suggest that the upper and the middle classes are able to place their cultural capital in the most favourable educational settings and their investments prove to be profitable in terms of generating social profits, but this was not the case for my mature students.

The reasons for selecting a certain college was also interesting. All of them based their choice of college on practicalities related to their commitments outside education.

Noreen spoke about her array of commitments:

> I suppose that when you are a mature student you have so much going on, that you have to also run the house and do your jobs, there's the kids, there's the football, there's the activities, there's the whole thing.

Time constraints determined geographical location of the HEI selected, and the students' lack of economic capital was also a factor. Ball (2003) proposes that mature students are not only constrained by personal finances but are also time-poor due to their numerous other commitments; for them, time is a valuable commodity. Reay (2002) suggests that the cost of travel and the time considerations were all primary elements in the decision-making process for mature students when they were selecting a college. The findings of this enquiry illuminate the challenges that mature students face on a daily basis identified as a main theme of 'balancing study, work and family commitments'. Consequently the college had to be in close proximity to minimize travelling time. According to Reay et al. (2002), the choices regarding where to study are limited and come down to looking at what they cannot have and then choosing from the few options left open to them. My cohort had an extremely limited choice of college. It had to be the nearest college that offered the undergraduate programme that interested them. One of the participants could only attend the one particular college because of her commitments to her children, but she would rather have studied elsewhere. The other five mature students were grateful that the undergraduate programme they were interested in was being offered in close proximity to their homes.

While many of the discourses surrounding WP address complex issues, it is seldom recognized how significant the material stresses are for people who are poor. The mature students in my study all identified themselves as being financially under stress and all had employment considerations to attend to on top of their study commitments.

This contrasts with the picture in most of the contemporary literature about how the transition to higher education and the decisions to be made look to most 16–19-year-olds. They had a robust sense of having a variety of choices when entering the field of higher education (Chisholm, 1995; Brynner et al., 1997; Furlong and Cartmel, 1997; Du Bois-Reymond, 1998; Ball et al., 2000).

Ivan spoke about his choice:

> This college was first on the list. I think it was because it was convenient and it was a bit closer. Financially I wouldn't have been able to manage if it were far away.

The mature students made their decisions pragmatically. However, it is the lack of economic capital that severely limits their choices. All identified themselves as being from working-class backgrounds and inherent throughout their narratives was their shortage of economic capital. Bourdieu has observed that economic capital is of great significance in the lives of students and suggests that it is the most powerful form of capital, as all are intrinsically linked to it. Lack of economic capital diminishes forms of social and cultural capital. With no money to spare, students cannot avail themselves of extracurricular activities or social networking. My students used words like 'busy', 'juggling' and 'sacrifice' to describe their lives. They felt they had more commitments outside their academic life than the traditional student. The reality of this situation meant they found themselves 'prioritising all the time', sacrificing certain elements of their lives to focus on study. Reay et al. (2002: 10) report that mature students sacrifice any social life or time for 'care of self'. Although my cohort don't talk about having no time for self-care, it is implicit within their narratives and the busy schedules they have to manage. This suggests that they have no opportunity to develop beneficial friendships and cultivate social networks within the academic setting. They talked about the necessity to work while they were in college to support themselves and their children, and four out of the six had dependent children, while one was the primary carer for his dependent elderly father. The findings highlighted that the students were prioritizing and juggling their academic commitments with their employment and caring responsibilities. Thus their lack of economic capital shaped their experiences of higher education.

All spoke about the sacrifices they made, especially around the time of examinations or submitting assignments. The huge demands these assessment obligations make on the mature students and the levels of stress they experience can scarcely be overstated. Fleming et al. (2010) found that mature students have to curtail their regular family activities so they can get through their academic courses. The findings from this enquiry concur with contemporary research showing my students prioritize their study at important times such as examinations or when assignments are due for submission (Reay et al., 2002; Fleming and Finnegan, 2011; Wright, 2011).

The sub-theme of 'attendance' was significant to my students. They spoke about feeling anxious if they missed a lecture or could not attend college fearing they would be unable to catch up. The concept of cultural capital explains this fear: their lack of assurance in their academic abilities, probably linked to their earlier educational difficulties, leaves them without the cultural capital to navigate the field of higher education with confidence. The pressures of attendance plus limited economic capital means they have to surmount grave social, personal and financial impediments to attend college (Fleming and Finnegan, 2011). Yet their life experience proved to be a positive force too, enabling them to cope with the challenges of higher education. This long survival in hard times can be viewed as a form of capital that such students use to their advantage. Some observers contend that experiences of disadvantage and early educational failure could actually motivate people to succeed academically.

The main theme of 'supportive networks' was explored throughout the narratives and analysed through the concept of social capital which, as Bourdieu notes, is particularly significant within the field of higher education. Social capital as a concept indicates the sum of resources a person has at their disposal that in some way ingratiates them within the field and gives them an advantage. Because those who lack social capital are at a disadvantage, social inequality is reproduced. Bourdieu (1986) saw social capital as ensuring that the elite were protected and the wrong type of person did not enter their circles. Importantly, then, social capital is used to exclude, divide and to reproduce social inequality. The narratives of these mature students showed clearly that this form of networking and amassing social capital was not afforded to them.

The social capital they did manage to amass was helpful as the students' narratives show the sub-themes 'support at home', 'importance of friends' and 'support staff within the college'. Such forms of social capital were significant in enabling the students to succeed. They received support at home from their immediate family, spouses and partners, that was of great consequence to them and were the obverse of their earlier experiences. Fleming and Finnegan (2011) found that family bestowing emotional and financial support was one of the key indicators for mature students' success. Wright (2011) describes the support of partners as essential, distinguishing between practical and emotional support. Similarly, my students talk about both emotional and practical support from partners and consider them as being of equal importance. They also mention receiving emotional support from friends and family and practical support that enables them to study at ease. They identify informal supports too, such as their fellow students, which made their classes positive experiences.

Bourdieu acknowledges that friends are a significant form of social capital in that they not only ease loneliness but add to a person's feeling of self-worth. This is reflected in the students' comments on the 'importance of friends' – so much so that they felt they wouldn't have been able to complete the course without them. Fleming and Finnegan (2011) found that peer support for mature students academically, emotionally and socially is a significant factor in success. Wright (2011: 91) also writes about the friendships formed but also about supportive pairs or 'study buddies'. The findings from this enquiry highlight this as a form of social capital that the students used to their advantage as they shared notes and resources and studied together in college and in their homes. The supportive networks they identified as their groups or friends had positive effects. Support staff were also positively viewed, and they appreciated the work of the disability officer, specifically recounting how they found her guidance and care an enormous support. These support networks and structures are identified through the analysis of the narratives as social capital. One of the mature students who refused to access the help of the disability officer on account of her earlier negative experiences with such staff was able to access the supports and resources through her friends who used the services. This was a way for her to amass social capital for herself when her friends shared the special resources. The students were inventive about creating ways of amassing and conveying social capital. But it is salient to note that none of them had any suggestions about how support might be improved for them. Clearly they did not fully identify the support as enhancing their social capital and engaging more with the totality of college life that their other commitments kept them from taking part in.

## Field

Education is a place of multifaceted processes. Bourdieu suggests that to comprehend interactions between people or understand an event or social phenomenon, it is essential to examine the social space in which these occur. The social space he refers to is the field. Employing the conceptual tool of field allows for the analysis of the field of higher education within this enquiry. Bourdieu (1998: 40) defines a field as 'a structured social space, a field of forces, a force field'. It is, therefore, a place of struggle, competition and a place of power. According to Bourdieu and Passeron (1977), the field of education reproduces itself more than other fields, and those that benefit from it are already possessed of social and economic advantages.

Within the field are people who are dominated and people who dominate. Agents within the field employ various strategies to succeed as they struggle to maintain their position. The concept of capital is helpful when examining the position of people within a given field as it places them in a position of advantage or disadvantage. This was evident in the narratives of the mature students when they spoke about entering the field of higher education and especially their experiences of the first year. They recognized that they had insufficient knowledge of what it would entail and what was expected of them academically. The field was alien to them. They were also at a disadvantage as to their standing within the field as their narratives revealed their lack of relevant cultural, social and economic capital. Their position within the field was not equal to that of traditional students and therefore they had a sense of inequality reproduced within the field.

The organizational structures of the field of higher education did not consider the specific needs of the mature student and the complex multifactor issues; their lack of economic capital and having to balance domestic obligations are not addressed within the field. Higher education does not take into account the busy lives of the mature student. It makes no allowances or concessions to ensure that their lives could be more manageable. The pressure of academic work, attendance at lectures and the lack – or cost – of childcare facilities makes life for the mature student much more stressful. Consultation around submission deadlines and timetabling of examinations is scarce and the students' voice is rarely heard in relation to the timetabling of lectures. Extracurricular activities are held mainly after the end of the college day, making it virtually impossible for mature students to attend. The students spoke about the challenges of balancing their busy lives. The sub-theme of 'attendance' was crucial to their overall experience. However this was not recognized and organizationally there were issues with timetables that could have been addressed to enable them to balance their academic life with their domestic obligations.

The findings of this enquiry suggest that the organizational structures of the field of higher education disadvantage mature students and limit their capabilities to amass social and cultural capital. The field further diminished their economic capital as the students explained. They face the prohibitive cost of attendance on a daily basis. Although there are no fees for attendance at higher education, there is a registration fee that has steadily increased since its introduction, making a lack of economic capital a serious issue.

The link between field and the relational structures of capital and habitus is inherent in the themes identified within the narratives. This can be understood through the relationship between field, capital and habitus as through careful analysis of the narratives it was demonstrated that there was a 'field–habitus match or clash' (Maton, 2008: 59).

The field–habitus clash was identified particularly in relation to these students' experiences of the compulsory educational sector. Bourdieu intimates that those who maintain the pre-existing order may do so without actually realizing that they are complicit. Thus teachers who were unaware of the disconnection for the mature students caused by their personal cognitive habitus and the institutional habitus inherent in the field, enabled the cycle of disadvantage to continue. However, in the theme identified as 'pleasant surprise', we see that the lecturers who were aware of the cognitive habitus of the mature students worked within the field to overcome this clash. They worked with the mature students in a spirit of shared learning and self-determination, appreciating the personal and cognitive habitus of these students.

Families use the field of education as a strategy to enhance their social position. The narratives make clear that the students valued the field of higher education, where they could advance their careers and personal development. However, their choices were curtailed by their domestic obligations. The field of education sorts and sifts people into various educational trajectories and different HEIs and this, suggested Bourdieu (1996), made it possible to produce elite institutes and the rest, thus enabling reproduction and social inequality within the field.

My findings illustrate how the economic, domestic and social obligations of the mature student dictated their educational trajectory and their choice of institute for study. The field of higher education is therefore part of the reproduction of social inequality.

Some of the mature students entered the field of higher education to improve their literacy skills, particularly the four whose skills were poor. Engaging with higher education enabled them to escape the shame and uncertainty they had felt. All expressed the notion that the process of education – learning for the sake of learning itself – was of prime importance. In direct contrast to their earlier educational experiences, the higher education provided a safe and enjoyable place for learning. Wright (2011) suggests that where poor educational practices are poor, there is a failure to address power issues between teachers and students. We saw this in the case of the mature students' earlier educational experiences. It is the organizational structures within the field of education and their rigid enforcement – for example, academic streaming – that contributed to the negative school experiences of the mature students.

Compulsory education offers support classes and services to students who have a diagnosed identified learning need. The three students in my cohort who were offered support classes found these classes to be entirely negative. They did not encompass individual learning plans and did not meet the students' academic needs. All three students recounted that they felt stigmatized for attending and were bullied by their classmates. Moreover, the classes were unhelpful and so damaging to their self-esteem that they voluntarily excluded themselves.

The consequent loss of appropriate learning supports compounded the students' overall struggle within school. They are living examples of what Bourdieu and Passeron (1979) describe as numerous acts of symbolic violence perpetrated by the field of education on the students it had no interest in helping to achieve their potential.

In contrast those within the field of higher education were satisfied with the supports they received there. However, one of the students excluded herself from these supports due to her earlier negative experiences, which illustrates the lasting effect of negative experiences throughout life. In the HEI, supports within the field were structured to be individualized and meet the varied needs of the students. Staff were respectful and delivered the service in a supportive and appropriate manner. The students spoke in glowing terms of the support staff and particularly the disability officer. Ivan said:

> Ahh well the fact that you have Maggie makes a huge difference, oh yeh she's a great support and she is brilliant at her job.

This is so heartening to hear. All is not lost: there is a happy ending to these students' stories. They immersed themselves in their new-found learning, they made strong friendships and discovered within themselves resilience, happiness and appreciation of the field of education. They grew not only in knowledge within their chosen field, but also in confidence. They were, as they themselves said, pleasantly surprised by their experiences of higher education.

The theoretical framework of habitus, capital and field (Bourdieu, 1984, 1990a) provide the analytical tools to understand and illuminate the impact of social inequality on the lives of mature students within the field of higher education. When describing their experiences they mentioned many commonalities that threaded significantly throughout their narratives. They recounted experiences of early education and secondary education, home and background characteristics, family support, relationships with teachers and their struggle to manage their many challenges. Their negative experiences of compulsory education influenced the decisions they made and how they experienced higher education at a later stage. It remains clear that the lack of cultural, social and economic capital and the mismatch between habitus and the educational field had nevertheless delivered negative experiences to my participants.

However, the experiences of all the mature students when within the field of higher education were positive. This appears to be due to the supportive networks they had at that time and the social capital they managed to amass. Of equal importance here are the lecturers themselves, their teaching styles and their non-judgemental approach, which ensured that the mature students felt that their habitus were aligned with the field of higher education. The students described simple examples of how they were made to feel valued by the lecturing and support staff, and it is these things that made the difference to the students' experience. The analytical tools of habitus, capital and field have enabled a comprehensive understanding of the experiences of the mature students and also of the impact of context and history in relation to present-day experiences of the field of higher education.

# Epilogue

Conducting our research was an enlightening journey for us both. Following the educational trajectories of people through the medium of narrative is a privilege and an honour. The stories the students told with such honesty and dignity enabled us as researchers to reflect upon our own practice and the educational practices and policies within our own countries of origin, in the UK and around the world. It highlighted the inequalities within the educational system but also illustrated the strength of character our participants showed, their tenacity and their drive to succeed in a world that presented them with so many challenges.

As educationalists within the field, our studies have illuminated the challenges faced by cohorts of students and made us more aware of the struggles of many potential students and the importance of a more balanced and reflective system that can meet the needs of all students justly and equitably.

## Reflections on our studies

Firstly, this book set out to understand and explain the issues of education, gender and social class, while also showing how concepts of culture have been salient in accessing higher education. Secondly, it has explored and evaluated Bourdieu's theories of cultural and social reproduction. The two studies focus on:

- how the existing education system and the lack of infrastructure impede access to higher education opportunities, such as situating HEIs in urban areas
- the strong hold of patriarchy that defines male domination in two distant and distinct contexts
- how women and the poor have a subordinate and under-privileged role, and how this can reinforce the existing gender and class dominance. The silence of one is the strength of the other
- how our participants are conforming to the status quo. They do not have the courage to challenge the prevailing norms of their societies. They realize the importance of education, money, power and social

status and make no attempt to overthrow it, merely to acquire a small share
- how the families' preference to early marriage instead of higher education is led by family pressures.

The studies illuminate the challenges faced by mature students within the field of higher education. Each gives an account of a group of disadvantaged students' personal struggle to climb the social hierarchy and empower themselves through education. Both studies demonstrate that cultural capital is more valuable than all the other forms of capital and, within that, the significance of education.

In the theoretical aspects of our studies, we conclude that the economic status of the people has a pivotal role in their access in education. Rich people with prominent economic capital are more likely to educate their children in elite institutions so as to accumulate cultural capital, tend to establish social circles as a strategy to reap benefits (social capital) and are well regarded and respected by others who value their capital (symbolic capital) (Bourdieu et al., 1999). Cultural capital and cultural reproduction theories are clearly applicable in Pakistan as much as they are in Ireland or anywhere in the world, where social reproduction is obvious.

Within the culture of education in both the Irish and the Pakistani contexts, the concepts of cultural capital and economic capital are so closely intertwined that it is difficult to separate one from the other in an attempt to distinguish which has a greater influence over the educational trajectory of an under-represented cohort within the field of higher education. The parents' and elders' cultural capital – the education they received and their attitudes – help to determine the decisions they make about the education of their children. Sadly, in the field our participants belong to, education of women is always considered less important than education of men, even though mothers are better positioned than fathers to pass on education (cultural capital) to their children, including boys. We see in one case how this impedes educational and economic advancement over generations until one woman, Shabana, breaks the vicious circle. A beautiful poem titled '*Chand roz aur, Meri Jaan! Faqat chand hi roz*', by Faiz Ahmed Faiz (1911–84) captures the crippling situation.

| | |
|---|---|
| *Zulm ki chaaon me dum lene pe majboor hain hum,*<br>*Aur kuch der sitam seh lein, Tadap lein, Ro lein,*<br>*Apne ajdaad ki miraas hai,*<br>*M'aazoor hain hum,*<br>*Jism par qaid hai, Jazbaat pe zanjeerein hain,*<br>*Fikr mahboos hai, Guftaar pe t'aazirein hain,*<br>*Apni himmat hai keh hum phir bhi jiye jaate hain,*<br>*Zindagi kya kisi musflis ki qaba hai jis mein,*<br>*Har gharry dard ke paivand lage jaate hain,*<br>*Lekin ab zulm ki mai'aad ke din thode hain,*<br>*Ik zara sabr ki faryaad ke din thode hain,*<br>*Arsa-e-dehr ki jhulsi hui weeraani mein,*<br>*Hum ko rehna hai par yoon hi toh nahi rehna,*<br>*Ajnabi haathon ka benaam garaan-baar sitam,*<br>*Aaj sehna hai, Hamesha toh nahin sehna hai.* | We are forced to stay in the shadow of injustice<br>It is inherited from our ancestors, so we are handicapped<br>Body is imprisoned, emotions chained<br>Thoughts are captive, and Words enslaved<br>Despite all, our strength keeps us alive<br>Is life the clothing of the poor,<br>In which we stitch a piece of worry every now and then<br>But now the days of rule of tyranny are few<br>And so are the days of Patience<br>In the long-lasting desert<br>We have to survive but not in the way we are<br>We have to bear the tyranny of fate<br>But we are not ready to bear it forever. |

The notion of habitus has also been important for our theoretical position: even in the most extreme conditions of life there seems to be space for individual choice. But choice is limited by the social structures within which people live. People all face social constraints, but they handle them in different ways. Human behaviour is, therefore, partly determined by structure and partly by choice. Habitus is a product of early socialization but it changes with later experiences. This feature of habitus makes it creative, and not just a set of rigid rules. The tendency of habitus to be in constant flux, to be ever-changing, makes it a method of analysis (Reay, 1995a, 2004). Bourdieu's framework explained the power struggle in the field, with the symbolic violence inflicted upon our participants both at home and in society. In their struggle, the students transformed their habitus to acquire more symbolic capital. Habitus is therefore at the heart of both our studies. We used habitus with the understanding that it adapts and accommodates, and also transforms itself (Reay, 1995b).

Habitus and cultural capital are conceptual tools that reveal a blend of possibilities, promises and problems for examining and interpreting the lives of our participants. It is the examination of the cognitive habitus of our participants and the lack of fit with the field of education that highlights the reproduction of the institution of education itself.

## Higher education as an instrument of social change around the world

Working in our far-flung countries, we each noted that education in general and higher education in particular are recognized as instruments for social change, youth empowerment and women's emancipation. In both countries, it has been the class system, patriarchy and an ineffective education system that were the main impediments to higher education. Cultural norms have a stronger hold than religion on the people. Neither men nor women are generally able to access higher education without the support of their families. Both our studies revealed the complex and paradoxical role of family support.

Through the voices of our participants, our studies demonstrate that participation in higher education brings many benefits and much empowerment. Engagement in higher education equips the poor, women and mature students with the knowledge that will form the basis of their economic independence and thus enable them to make decisions about their own lives.

## Implications

Those who took part in our studies gained insights into the ways class and gender inequalities are perpetuated and discovered ways of subverting the process. We hope that many more such studies will be conducted and that non-traditional and poor students see themselves and can be seen and heard in the world.

Since our studies are based on qualitative data and we treated and presented our participants as individuals, they should not be thought of as universal. We researched their individuality. The main purpose of ethnographic study is to give voice to people. Our aim is that our reader hears the voices of common men and women in the contexts of the East and the West, and thus understands how people in the developing and developed world share similar issues in their personal lives. We aim especially for this book to bring these issues of education to the attention of the wider academic community.

We hope our studies will help readers understand the living conditions of underprivileged people in Pakistan and in rural Ireland. We further provide concrete examples of the efforts and struggles that ordinary people throughout the world have to make to improve their living conditions. We say 'throughout the world' because what is happening in our research contexts is just one manifestation of what happens in many countries and has often found powerful expression in literary works, for example Frantz Fanon's *The Wretched of the Earth* for Algeria, Mariano Azuela's *The Underdogs* (*Los de abajo*) for Mexico, and José Rizal's novel *Noli me tangere* (*Don't Touch Me*) for the Philippines. We show how social structures, policies and practices created by the dominant people to serve their purpose have an impact on the experiences of the subjugated. Such insights could prove particularly valuable.

Pakistani and Irish societies have complex structures, employing heterogeneous criteria of social differentiation, of which class, gender, religion, language and the rural–urban dichotomy are easily visible. We did not explore any of these in depth. There is, therefore, scope for future research taking different directions. Future scholars might like to explore the significance of religion, ethnicity or socio-economic class in relation to access and WP within the field of higher education.

Our studies raised certain issues that can be addressed in future research, for example:

- rights versus duties
- choices in decision making
- children's lack of interest in education
- parents' lack of support of children who want to study
- the significance of curricular, co-curricular and extracurricular activities
- the importance of appropriate supports for mature students, such as childcare facilities, and student-centred timetabling.

Future studies might usefully explore large social issues, like the feudal system, the different quality of education provided by private and government schools, by schools in cities and in villages or the medium of instruction and language empowerment.

## Concluding remarks

The most important part of our studies are our participants. They come from different backgrounds and some of them heroically try to pull themselves up by their bootstraps out of the morass they are in. The studies rest on the emotional moments in interviews when participants laughed with joy or shed tears while telling their stories. Their enthusiasm, eagerness and their seriousness in telling the best and worst of their experiences showed their willingness to tell the world about their lives. Nobody had given them a chance to speak before so no one had ever heard them before. They highlight their hardships and struggles due to patriarchy, poverty and gender discrimination. The family and village or community might or might not be supportive, but all had to forge their own path and their own fortune. Our participants continued to advance towards better living conditions because their desire was strong enough to overcome all obstacles. For each of them, education was a stepping stone to a more satisfying life, and it helped them to improve their social standing and that of their families.

We end with the echoing words of our Sindhi participant, Shabana, spoken to her mother at the time of her divorce case:

> Do not worry *Amma* [mother], let all the worries be mine.
> Forget about me. Think that you never gave birth to a daughter.
> Or think that the daughter to whom you gave birth is not linked to you anymore.
> Do not worry about what the neighbours might say to you about me.
> What do they know about your anguish or mine!
> Forget about them and their heartless gossip. People are merciless.
> You have done what you could in bringing me up. I love you, *Amma*.
> Do not think about what will happen to me.
> Do not worry about the future. Forget our disagreements.
> Let things be. Let me take care and decide. I love you.

# References

Ahmad, A. (1988) کیا ہم اکٹھے رہ سکتے ہیں؟ پاکستان میں قومیاتی مسئلے کا تجزیہ *Kya Hum Ikathay Reh Sakte Hain? Pakistan mein Qaumiyati Masalay ka Tajzia* [in Urdu] (translation: Can We Live Together? An Analysis of the Ethnic Problems in Pakistan). Lahore: Maktaba Fikr o Danish.

Alasuutari, P. (1995) *Researching Culture: Qualitative method and cultural studies*. London: SAGE Publications.

Alasuutari, P. (1998) *An Invitation to Social Research*. London: SAGE Publications.

Archer, L. (2003) 'Social class and higher education'. In Archer, L., Hutchings, M., Ross, A., Leathwood, C., Gilchrist, R. and Phillips, D., *Higher Education and Social Class: Issues of exclusion and inclusion*. London: RoutledgeFalmer, 5–20.

Bakhtin, M.M. (1981) *The Dialogic Imagination: Four essays*. Ed. Holquist, M. Trans. Emerson, C. and Holquist, M. Austin: University of Texas Press.

Ball, S.J. (2003) *Class Strategies and the Education Market: The middle classes and social advantage*. London: RoutledgeFalmer.

Ball, S.J., Maguire, M. and Macrae, S. (2000) *Choice, Pathways and Transitions Post-16: New youth, new economies in the global city*. London: RoutledgeFalmer.

Barthes, R. (1977) *Image, Music, Text*. Trans. Heath, S. New York: Hill and Wang.

Bassnett, S. (2002) *Translation Studies*. 3rd ed. London: Routledge.

Behan, J. and Shally, C. (2010) *Occupational Employment Forecasts 2015* (FÁS/ESRI Manpower Forecasting Studies Report 13). Dublin: Skills and Labour Market Research Unit.

Benjamin, W. (1969) *Illuminations*. Ed. Arendt, H. Trans. Zohn, H. New York: Schocken Books.

Blanden, J. and Machin, S. (2004) 'Educational inequality and the expansion of UK higher education'. *Scottish Journal of Political Economy*, 51 (2), 230–49.

Blumer, H. (1969) *Symbolic Interactionism: Perspective and method*. Englewood Cliffs, NJ: Prentice-Hall.

Bogenschneider, K. (1997) 'Parental involvement in adolescent schooling: A proximal process with transcontextual validity'. *Journal of Marriage and Family*, 59 (3), 718–33.

Bourdieu, P. (1977) *Outline of a Theory of Practice*. Trans. Nice, R. Cambridge: Cambridge University Press.

Bourdieu, P. (1981) 'Systems of education and systems of thought'. In Young, M.F.D. (ed.), *Knowledge and Control: New directions for the sociology of education*. London: Collier-Macmillan, 189–209.

Bourdieu, P. (1984) *Distinction: A social critique of the judgement of taste*. Trans. Nice, R. Cambridge, MA: Harvard University Press.

Bourdieu, P. (1986) 'The forms of capital'. In Richardson, J.G. (ed.), *Handbook of Theory and Research for the Sociology of Education*. New York: Greenwood Press, 241–58.

Bourdieu, P. (1988) *Homo Academicus*. Trans. Collier, P. Cambridge: Polity Press.

Bourdieu, P. (1990a) *The Logic of Practice*. Trans. Nice, R. Cambridge: Polity Press.

Bourdieu, P. (1990b) *In Other Words: Essays towards a reflexive sociology*. Trans. Adamson, M. Cambridge: Polity Press.

Bourdieu, P. (1993) *The Field of Cultural Production: Essays on art and literature*. Ed. Johnson, R. Cambridge: Polity Press.

Bourdieu, P. (1998) *Practical Reason: On the theory of action*. Stanford: Stanford University Press.

Bourdieu, P. and Passeron, J.-C. (1977) *Reproduction in Education, Society and Culture*. Trans. Nice, R. London: SAGE Publications.

Bourdieu, P. and Passeron, J.-C. (1979) *The Inheritors: French students and their relation to culture*. Trans. Nice, R. Chicago: University of Chicago Press.

Bourdieu, P. and Passeron, J.-C. (1990) *Reproduction in Education, Society and Culture*. Trans. Nice, R. Rev. ed. London: SAGE Publications.

Bourdieu, P. and Wacquant, L.J.D. (1992) *An Invitation to Reflexive Sociology*. Cambridge: Polity Press.

Bourdieu, P. et al. (1999) *The Weight of the World: Social suffering in contemporary society*. Trans. Pankhurst Ferguson, P. Stanford: Stanford University Press.

Bourner, T., Hamed, M., Barnett, R. and Reynolds, A. (1988) *Students on CNAA's Part-Time First Degree Courses: Summary report* (CNAA Development Services Publication 16). London: Council for National Academic Awards.

Bowl, M. (2001) 'Experiencing the barriers: Non-traditional students entering higher education'. *Research Papers in Education*, 16 (2), 141–60.

Bowles, S. and Gintis, H. (2002) 'The inheritance of inequality'. *Journal of Economic Perspectives*, 16 (3), 3–30.

Brooks, R. (2003) 'Young people's higher education choices: The role of family and friends'. *British Journal of Sociology of Education*, 24 (3), 283–97.

Brooks, R. (2008) 'Accessing higher education: The influence of cultural and social capital on university choice'. *Sociology Compass*, 2 (4), 1355–71.

Broomfield, C. (1993) 'The importance of mature, part-time students to higher education in the UK'. *Higher Education*, 25 (2), 189–205.

Bruyn, S.T. (1966) *The Human Perspective in Sociology: The methodology of participant observation*. Englewood Cliffs, NJ: Prentice-Hall.

Burke, P.J. (2002) *Accessing Education: Effectively widening participation*. Stoke-on-Trent: Trentham Books.

Bynner, J., Ferri, E. and Shepherd, P. (eds) (1997) *Twenty-Something in the 1990s: Getting on, getting by, getting nowhere*. Aldershot: Ashgate.

Catford, J.C. (1965) *A Linguistic Theory of Translation: An essay in applied linguistics*. London: Oxford University Press.

Charmaz, K. (1995) 'Between positivism and postmodernism: Implications for methods'. *Studies in Symbolic Interaction*, 17, 43–72.

Chisholm, L. (1995) 'Cultural semantics: Occupations and gender discourse'. In Atkinson, P., Davies, B. and Delamont, S. (eds), *Discourse and Reproduction: Essays in honor of Basil Bernstein*. Cresskill, NJ: Hampton Press, 25–50.

Clancy, P. (2001) *College Entry in Focus: A fourth national survey of access to higher education*. Dublin: Higher Education Authority.

Clandinin, D.J. and Connelly, F.M. (2000) *Narrative Enquiry: Experience and story in qualitative research*. San Francisco: Jossey-Bass.

Clifford, J. (1988) *The Predicament of Culture: Twentieth-century ethnography, literature, and art*. Cambridge, MA: Harvard University Press.

Clifford, J. and Marcus, G.E. (eds) (1986) *Writing Culture: The poetics and politics of ethnography*. Berkeley: University of California Press.

Collins, J. (1993) 'Determination and contradiction: An appreciation and critique of the work of Pierre Bourdieu on language and education'. In Calhoun, C., LiPuma, E. and Postone, M. (eds), *Bourdieu: Critical perspectives*. Cambridge: Polity Press, 116–38.

Connelly, F.M. and Clandinin, D.J. (1990) 'Stories of experience and narrative enquiry'. *Educational Researcher*, 19 (5), 2–14.

Cree, V., Hounsell, J., Christie, H., McCune, V. and Tett, L. (2009) 'From further education to higher education: Social work students' experiences of transition to an ancient, research-led university'. *Social Work Education*, 28 (8), 887–901.

Creswell, J.W. (2007) *Qualitative Inquiry and Research Design: Choosing among five approaches*. 2nd ed. Thousand Oaks, CA: SAGE Publications.

Davies, B. (1982) *Life in the Classroom and Playground: The accounts of primary school children*. London: Routledge and Kegan Paul.

Davies, P., Osborne, M. and Williams, J. (2002) *For Me or Not for Me? That is the Question: A study of mature students' decision making and higher education* (Research Report 297). London: Department for Education and Skills.

Davies, P. and Williams, J. (2001) 'For me or not for me? Fragility and risk in mature students' decision-making'. *Higher Education Quarterly*, 55 (2), 185–203.

Denzin, N.K. (1991) 'Representing lived experiences in ethnographic texts'. *Studies in Symbolic Interaction*, 12, 59–70.

Devine, F. (2004) *Class Practices: How parents help their children get good jobs*. Cambridge: Cambridge University Press.

Ding, H. (2008) 'Living through Ambiguity: The cross-cultural experience of Chinese students in London'. Unpublished PhD thesis, Goldsmiths, University of London.

du Bois-Reymond, M. (1998) '"I don't want to commit myself yet": Young people's life concepts'. *Journal of Youth Studies*, 1 (1), 63–79.

Dumais, S.A. (2002) 'Cultural capital, gender, and school success: The role of habitus'. *Sociology of Education*, 75 (1), 44–68.

Duru-Bellat, M. (2008) 'Recent trends in social reproduction in France: Should the political promises of education be revisited?'. *Journal of Education Policy*, 23 (1), 81–95.

Edwards, A. and Talbot, R. (1994) *The Hard-Pressed Researcher: A research handbook for the caring professions*. London: Longman.

Edwards, R. (1993) *Mature Women Students: Separating or connecting family and education*. London: Taylor and Francis.

Edwards, R. (2004) 'Present and absent in troubling ways: Families and social capital debates'. *Sociological Review*, 52 (1), 1–21.

Elbaz-Luwisch, F. (1997) 'Narrative research: Political issues and implications'. *Teaching and Teacher Education*, 13 (1), 75–83.

Feagin, J.R., Orum, A.M. and Sjoberg, G. (eds) (1991), *A Case for the Case Study*. Chapel Hill: University of North Carolina Press.

Fleming, T. and Finnegan, F. (2011) *Non-traditional Students in Higher Education: A research report*. RANLHE, University of Wroclaw. Available at: http://www.dsw.edu.pl/fileadmin/www-ranlhe/index.html.

Fleming, T., Loxley, A., Kenny, A. and Finnegan, F. (2010) *Where Next? Mapping and understanding the post first degree destinations of mature disadvantaged students in three third level institutions*. Dublin: Combat Poverty Agency.

Flowerdew, J. and Miller, L. (2008) 'Social structure and individual agency in second language learning: Evidence from three life histories'. *Critical Inquiry in Language Studies* 5 (4), 201–24.

Forster, E.M. (1973) *Howards' End*. Edited by Oliver Stallybrass. Harmondsworth: Penguin Modern Classics.

Fowler, B. (1996) 'An introduction to Pierre Bourdieu's "understanding"'. *Theory, Culture and Society*, 13 (2), 1–16.

Francis, H. (1993) 'Advancing phenomenography: Questions of method'. *Nordisk Pedagogik*, 13 (2), 68–75.

Freeman, M. (1984) 'History, narrative, and life-span developmental knowledge'. *Human Development*, 27 (1), 1–19.

Fries, C.J. (2009) 'Bourdieu's reflexive sociology as a theoretical basis for mixed methods research: An application to complementary and alternative medicine'. *Journal of Mixed Methods Research*, 3 (4), 326–48.

Furlong, A. and Cartmel, F. (1997) *Young People and Social Change: Individualization and risk in late modernity*. Buckingham: Open University Press.

Gayer, L. (2014) *Karachi: Ordered disorder and the struggle for the city*. New York: Oxford University Press.

Geertz, C. (1988) *Works and Lives: The anthropologist as author*. Stanford: Stanford University Press.

Grenfell, M. (2004) *Pierre Bourdieu: Agent provocateur*. London: Continuum.

Grenfell, M. (ed.) (2008) *Pierre Bourdieu: Key concepts*. Stocksfield: Acumen.

Grenfell, M., James, D., Hodkinson, P., Reay, D. and Robbins, D. (2004) *Bourdieu and Education: Acts of practical theory*. Taylor and Francis eBooks.

Hamers, J.J. and Blanc, M.A.F. (2000) *Bilinguality and Bilingualism*. 2nd edn. Cambridge: Cambridge University Press.

Hammersley, M. (1994) 'Introducing ethnography'. In Graddol, D., Maybin, J. and Stierer, B. (eds), *Researching Language and Literacy in Social Context: A reader*. Clevedon: Multilingual Matters, 1–17.

Harré, R. and Secord, P.F. (1973) *The Explanation of Social Behaviour*. Totowa, NJ: Littlefield, Adams and Co.

Hart, P. (1996) 'Problematizing enquiry in environmental education: Issues of method in a study of teacher thinking and practice'. *Canadian Journal of Environmental Education*, 1, 56–88.

HEA (Higher Education Authority) (2011) *National Strategy for Higher Education to 2030*. Department for Education and Skills (Dublin), available at: http://hea.ie/assets/uploads/2017/06/National-Strategy-for-Higher-Education-2030.pdf.

HEA (Higher Education Authority) (2012) *Towards a Future Higher Education Landscape* (Consultation Document), available at: http://hea.ie/assets/uploads/2017/04/Towards-a-Higher-Education-Landscape.pdf.

HEA (Higher Education Authority) (2015) *National Plan for Equity of Access to Higher Education 2015–2019*. Dublin: Higher Education Authority.

Henry, M., Knight, J., Lingard, R. and Taylor, S. (1988) *Understanding Schooling: An introductory sociology of Australian education*. Sydney: Routledge.

Jenkins, R. (2002) *Key Sociologists: Pierre Bourdieu*. London: Routledge.

Joyo, M.I. (2005) *The Betrayal: Sindh bides the day of freedom* (Vol. 1). Hyderabad: Sindhi Adeeban ji Sahkari Sangat.

Kamil, M.L., Langer, J.A. and Shanahan, T. (1985) *Understanding Reading and Writing Research*. Boston: Allyn and Bacon.

Kazi, A.A. (1987) *Ethnicity and Education in Nation-Building: The case of Pakistan*. Lanham, MD: University Press of America.

Kearney, C. (1998) 'Deep Excavations: An examination of the tangled roots of identity in modern cosmopolitan societies'. *International Journal of Inclusive Education*, 2 (4), 309–24.

Kearney, C. (2001) 'The Monkey's Mask: Identity, memory, narrative, voice'. Unpublished PhD thesis, Goldsmiths, University of London.

Kearney, C. (2003) *The Monkey's Mask: Identity, memory, narrative and voice*. Stoke-on-Trent: Trentham Books.

Kenway, J. and McLeod, J. (2004) 'Bourdieu's reflexive sociology and "spaces of points of view": Whose reflexivity, which perspective?'. *British Journal of Sociology of Education*, 25 (4), 525–44.

Kettley, N. (2007) 'The past, present and future of widening participation research'. *British Journal of Sociology of Education*, 28 (3), 333–47.

Khuhro, H. (1978) *The Making of Modern Sind: British policy and social change in the nineteenth century*. Karachi: Indus Publications.

Lareau, A. and Horvat, E.M. (1999) 'Moments of social inclusion and exclusion: Race, class, and cultural capital in family–school relationships'. *Sociology of Education*, 72 (1), 37–53.

Lejeune, P. (1989) *On Autobiography*. Ed. Eakin, P.J. Trans. Leary, K. Minneapolis: University of Minnesota Press.

Lin, A.M.Y. (1999) 'Doing-English-lessons in the reproduction or transformation of social worlds?'. *TESOL Quarterly*, 33 (3), 393–412.

Markovits, C. (2008) 'Urban society in colonial Sindh (1843–1947)'. In Boivin, M. (ed.), *Sindh through History and Representations: French contributions to Sindhi studies*. Karachi: Oxford University Press.

Marton, F. (1981) 'Phenomenography – describing conceptions of the world around us'. *Instructional Science*, 10 (2), 177–200.

Mathers, J. and Parry, J. (2010) 'Older mature students' experiences of applying to study medicine in England: An interview study'. *Medical Education*, 44 (11), 1084–94.

Maton, K. (2008) 'Habitus'. In Grenfell, M. (ed.), *Pierre Bourdieu: Key concepts*. Stocksfield: Acumen, 49–66.

McClelland, K. (1990) 'Cumulative disadvantage among the highly ambitious'. *Sociology of Education*, 63 (2), 102–21.

Miller, J. and Glassner, B. (2004) 'The "inside" and the "outside": Finding realities in interviews'. In Silverman, D. (ed.), *Qualitative Research: Theory, method and practice*. 2nd ed. London: SAGE Publications, 125–39.

Mills, C. and Gale, T. (2007) 'Researching social inequalities in education: Towards a Bourdieuian methodology'. *International Journal of Qualitative Studies in Education*, 20 (4), 433–47.

Mishler, E.G. (1986) *Research Interviewing: Context and narrative*. Cambridge, MA: Harvard University Press.

Moore, R. (2008) 'Capital'. In Grenfell, M. (ed.), *Pierre Bourdieu: Key concepts*. Stocksfield: Acumen, 101–17.

Morley, L. (1999) *Organising Feminisms: The micropolitics of the academy*. Basingstoke: Macmillan.

Nader, L. (1993) 'Paradigm busting and vertical linkage'. *Contemporary Sociology*, 22 (1), 6–7.

Obied, V.M. (2009) 'How do siblings shape the language environment in bilingual families?'. *International Journal of Bilingual Education and Bilingualism*, 12 (6), 705–20.

OECD (Organisation for Economic Co-operation and Development) (2006) *Review of National Policies for Education: Higher education in Ireland*. Paris: OECD Publishing.

OECD (Organisation for Economic Co-operation and Development) (2009) *Highlights from Education at a Glance 2009*. Paris: OECD Publishing.

Osborne, M., Marks, A. and Turner, E. (2004) 'Becoming a mature student: How adult applicants weigh the advantages and disadvantages of higher education'. *Higher Education*, 48 (3), 291–315.

O'Sullivan, J. (2015) 'Foreword'. In Higher Education Authority *National Plan for Equity of Access to Higher Education 2015–2019*. Dublin: Higher Education Authority, 1.

Pal, P. (ed.) (2008) *Sindh: Past glory, present nostalgia*. Delhi: Eastern Book Corporation.

Polkinghorne, D.E. (1988) *Narrative Knowing and the Human Sciences*. Albany: State University of New York Press.

Polkinghorne, D.E. (1995) 'Narrative configuration in qualitative analysis'. *Qualitative Studies in Education*, 8 (1), 5–23.

Rahman, T. (1996) *Language and Politics in Pakistan*. Karachi: Oxford University Press.

Rahman, T. (1999) *Language, Education and Culture*. Karachi: Oxford University Press.

Reay, D. (1995a) '"They employ cleaners to do that": Habitus in the primary classroom'. *British Journal of Sociology of Education*, 16 (3), 353–71.

Reay, D. (1995b) 'Mothers' Involvement in Primary Schooling: The influence of social class on home–school relations'. Unpublished PhD thesis, London South Bank University.

Reay, D. (1998) '"Always knowing" and "never being sure": Familial and institutional habituses and higher education choice'. *Journal of Education Policy*, 13 (4), 519–29.

Reay, D. (2000) 'A useful extension of Bourdieu's conceptual framework? Emotional capital as a way of understanding mothers' involvement in their children's education?'. *Sociological Review*, 48 (4), 568–85.

Reay, D. (2002) 'Class, authenticity and the transition to higher education for mature students'. *Sociological Review*, 50 (3), 398–418.

Reay, D. (2004) '"It's all becoming a habitus": Beyond the habitual use of habitus in educational research'. *British Journal of Sociology of Education*, 25 (4), 431–44.

Reay, D., Ball, S. and David, M. (2002) '"It's taking me a long time but I'll get there in the end": Mature students on access courses and higher education choice'. *British Educational Research Journal*, 28 (1), 5–19.

Reay, D., David, M. and Ball, S. (2001) 'Making a difference? Institutional habituses and higher education choice'. *Sociological Research Online*, 5 (4). Online. www.socresonline.org.uk/5/4/reay.html (accessed 22 August 2012).

Reay, D., David, M.E. and Ball, S. (2005) *Degrees of Choice: Social class, race and gender in higher education*. Stoke-on-Trent: Trentham Books.

Reay, D. and Mirza, H.S. (1997) 'Uncovering genealogies of the margins: Black supplementary schooling'. *British Journal of Sociology of Education*, 18 (4), 477–99.

Robinson, R.V. and Garnier, M.A. (1985) 'Class reproduction among men and women in France: Reproduction theory on its home ground'. *American Journal of Sociology*, 91 (2), 250–80.

Robson, C. (2002) *Real World Research: A resource for social scientists and practitioner-researchers*. 2nd ed. Oxford: Blackwell.

Rosen, H. (1998) *Speaking from Memory: The study of autobiographical discourse*. Stoke-on-Trent: Trentham Books.

Sapir, E. (1949) *Culture, Language and Personality: Selected essays*. Ed. Mandelbaum, D.G. Berkeley: University of California Press.

Sayer, A. (2005) 'Class, moral worth and recognition'. *Sociology*, 39 (5), 947–63.

Shahriar, A. (2012) 'Educational success and failure of learners from similar socio-cultural backgrounds: Two life story interviews'. *Educational Futures*, 4 (3), 39–57.

Shahriar, A. (2013a) 'Making a Better Life: The stories of people from poor rural backgrounds in Sindh, Pakistan'. Unpublished PhD thesis, Goldsmiths, University of London.

Shahriar, A. (2013b) 'How do some succeed against all odds?'. *International Journal of Learner Diversity and Identities*, 19 (3), 37–44.

Shahriar, A. (2015) 'Bourdieu's conceptual triad: It can be applied to as distinct a context as Pakistan'. *ARIEL*, 28, 1–20.

Shahriar, A., Baloch, S. and Bughio, F.A. (2014) 'Restraints on language and culture of Sindh: An historical perspective'. *Grassroots*, 48 (1), 29–42.

Shevlin, M., Kenny, M. and McNeela, E. (2004) 'Participation in higher education for students with disabilities: An Irish perspective'. *Disability and Society*, 19 (1), 15–30.

Siddiqui, H. (2006) *Education in Sindh Past and Present*. 2nd ed. Jamshoro: Institute of Sindhiology, University of Sindh.

Siraj (2009) *Sindhi Language*. Trans. Siraj, A. Hyderabad: Sindhi Language Authority.

Sjoberg, G., Williams, N., Vaughan, T.R. and Sjoberg, A.F. (1991) 'The case study approach in social research: Basic methodological issues'. In Feagin, J.R., Orum, A.M. and Sjoberg, G. (eds), *A Case for the Case Study*. Chapel Hill: University of North Carolina Press, 27–79.

Skehill, C. (2007) 'Researching the history of social work: Exposition of a history of the present approach'. *European Journal of Social Work*, 10 (4), 449–63.

Stevenson, D.L. and Baker, D.P. (1987) 'The family–school relation and the child's school performance'. *Child Development*, 58 (5), 1348–57.

Swartz, D. (1997) *Culture and Power: The sociology of Pierre Bourdieu*. Chicago: University of Chicago Press.

Syed, G.M. (1974) *Sindhi Culture* سنڌي ڪلچر [in Sindhi]. Karachi: Naeen Sindh Publication.

Taylor, M.J. (1981) *Caught Between: A review of research into the education of pupils of West Indian origin*. Windsor: National Foundation for Educational Research.

Thompson, J. (2000) 'Introduction'. In Thompson, J. (ed.), *Stretching the Academy: The politics and practice of widening participation in higher education*. Leicester: National Institute of Adult Continuing Education, 1–11.

Trow, M. (1973) *Problems in the Transition for Elite to Mass Higher Education*. Berkeley: Carnegie Commission on Higher Education.

Wacquant, L.J.D. (1998) 'Pierre Bourdieu'. In Stones, R. (ed.), *Key Sociological Thinkers*. New York: New York University Press, 215–29.

White, H. (1981) 'The value of narrativity in the representation of reality'. In Mitchell, W.J.T. (ed.), *On Narrative*. Chicago: University of Chicago Press, 1–12.

Williams, J. (ed.) (1997) *Negotiating Access to Higher Education: The discourse of selectivity and equity*. Buckingham: Society for Research into Higher Education and Open University Press.

Willis, P. (1978) *Learning to Labour: How working class kids get working class jobs*. Farnborough: Saxon House.

Woodley, A. (2001) 'Learning and earning: Measuring "rates of return" among mature graduates from part-time distance courses'. *Higher Education Quarterly*, 55 (1), 28–41.

Woodley, A. and Brennan, J. (2000) 'Higher education and graduate employment in the United Kingdom'. *European Journal of Education*, 35 (2), 239–49.

Woodley, A., Wagner, L., Slowly, M., Hamilton, M. and Fulton, O. (1987) *Choosing to Learn: Adults in education*. Buckingham: Society for Research into Higher Education and Open University Press.

Woods, P. (1999) *Successful Writing for Qualitative Researchers*. London: Routledge.

Wright, H.R. (2011) *Women Studying Childcare: Integrating lives through adult education*. Stoke-on-Trent: Trentham Books.

Yin, R.K. (2003) *Applications of Case Study Research*. 2nd ed. Thousand Oaks, CA: SAGE Publications.

# Index